D1066081

tapas STEP-BY-STEP

the perfect guide to Spain's small bites

tapas STEP-BY-STEP

the perfect guide to Spain's small bites

LOVE FOOD™

First published in 2013
LOVE FOOD is an imprint of Parragon Books Ltd

Parragon
Chartist House
15–17 Trim Street
Bath, BA1 1HA, UK

www.parragon.com/lovefood

ISBN: 978-1-4723-0724-8

Printed in China

Photography by Mike Cooper
Home economy by Lincoln Jefferson
Cover design by Geoff Borin; background texture © Getty Images
Internal design by Talking Design
Introduction and editing by Fiona Biggs
New recipes by Beverly LeBlanc

Notes for the Reader
This book uses both metric and imperial measurements. Follow the same units of measurement throughout; do not mix metric and imperial. All spoon measurements are level: teaspoons are assumed to be 5 ml, and tablespoons are assumed to be 15 ml. Unless otherwise stated, milk is assumed to be full fat, eggs and individual vegetables are medium, and pepper is freshly ground black pepper. Unless otherwise stated, all root vegetables should be washed in plain water and peeled prior to using.

Garnishes, decorations and serving suggestions are all optional and not necessarily included in the recipe ingredients or method.

The times given are an approximate guide only. Preparation times differ according to the techniques used by different people and the cooking times may also vary from those given. Optional ingredients, variations or serving suggestions have not been included in the time calculations.

Recipes using raw or very lightly cooked eggs should be avoided by infants, the elderly, pregnant women, convalescents and anyone suffering from an illness. Pregnant and breastfeeding women are advised to avoid eating peanuts and peanut products. Sufferers from nut allergies should be aware that some of the ready-made ingredients used in the recipes in this book may contain nuts. Always check the packaging before use.

Vegetarians should be aware that some of the ready-made ingredients used in the recipes in this book may contain animal products. Always check the packaging before use.

contents

introduction

This stunning cookbook, with its wealth of beautiful and immensely useful photographs, is the perfect introduction to Spanish tapas and will prove to be an invaluable and delightful addition to any cook's bookshelf. The recipes are straightforward, easy to follow, clearly illustrated, delicious and completely authentic, so whatever your level of expertise in the kitchen they provide all you need to whip up a whole range of tasty tapas dishes.

Every recipe starts with a photograph of all the ingredients, but this is more than just a pretty picture or – even less helpful – a montage that is not to scale, so that a chilli appears to be the same size as a red pepper. Instead, it serves as a handy way of checking that you have everything ready before you start cooking. Just comparing the picture with the ingredients arranged on your own worktop or kitchen table will ensure that you haven't missed anything out, and when it's time to add the parsley, for example, you have already chopped it as specified in the ingredients list. If you're uncertain how thinly to slice mushrooms, a glance at the photograph will provide an instant answer.

Each short and straightforward step of the method is clearly explained without any jargon or difficult technical terms. Once again, what you see in the photograph is what you should expect to see in front of you. Not only is this reassuring for the novice cook, those with more experience will also find it a helpful reminder of the little touches that can easily be overlooked. Each recipe ends with a mouthwatering photograph of the finished dish, complete with any serving suggestions.

why you need this book

The Spanish are masters of the informal, unplanned eating experience and tapas are an ideal way to share food and drink with friends in a casual and unhurried way. Because the Mediterranean diet is based on simply prepared, fresh food in season, a meal of tapas will be heavy on flavour and light on saturated fats.

In this book there are 60 fuss-free recipes that will enable you to re-create the authentic taste of food served in a tapas bar. You can pick and choose from the recipes to produce a range of tapas that best suits the occasion. You can tailor many of the recipes to suit your palate, using milder chillies if you don't like heavily spiced food, or adding stronger paprika if you like to feel the heat. Remember that tapas are not starters – the idea is to make a meal of five or six individual tapas, or two or three of the larger portions known as *raciones*. Mix and match from the range of meat and fish tapas, empanadas, tortillas and simple dishes of stuffed olives or toasted nuts, and you will feel as if you've just enjoyed a full meal.

top tips for success

> Before you start to cook, read your way through the entire recipe – ingredients list and method – so that you will know exactly what you need. Scrabbling around at the back of a cupboard to find a rarely used ingredient or, worse, finding that you don't have it in your storecupboard, is frustrating and can cause you to take your eye off the ball, leading to food being burnt or over-cooked. Do as much chopping, slicing and grinding as possible in advance.

> In an ideal world you would always have time to cook from scratch, but when you're pressed for time it's handy to have a supply of canned or bottled olives, whole almonds and other nuts, and artichoke hearts and grilled red peppers in oil. Any one of these will make a simple tapa, or they can

>1 >2 >3

>1>2>3

be combined with other ingredients for a more complex one. Do keep an eye on the expiry date of any nuts in your storecupboard. Their shelf life is limited – to extend it, you could keep them in the refrigerator.

> Take your lead from Spanish cooks and always buy fresh vegetables in season. Your tapas dishes will be more authentic if you combine ingredients that would be readily available together in a given season.

> When planning your tapas meal, remember that you will be serving everything at the same time, so plan carefully so that you're not stuck in the kitchen while everybody else is eating. It will make your life easier if you include some simple tapas that can go straight from jar, can or packet to serving dish (such as olives, grilled red peppers and almonds), as well as some dishes that require no cooking or ones that can be cooked ahead and served warm, at room temperature or cold. Limit any dishes that must be served hot to one or two, and choose at least one that is finished in the oven rather than on the hob.

> Oven-heating instructions usually appear at the start of the recipes for a reason – do make sure to preheat the oven and grill so that they are ready when you need to use them. A conventional oven can take up to 15 minutes to reach the required temperature.

> Be careful when cooking with oil and never leave the pan or deep-fat fryer unattended. If you are unavoidably called away while cooking, turn off the heat.

> Always use a good Spanish olive oil – its distinctive flavour will enhance all your tapas dishes. Keep a supply of different grades in a cool dark place, along with some Spanish sherry vinegar.

>4>5>6

useful equipment

baking dishes, baking sheet and roasting tins
You will need several of these in different sizes, ensuring that you always have the appropriate one for cooking or finishing off a dish in the oven.

knives
Good-quality, heavy, well-balanced knives are essential in any kitchen. Keep them sharp at all times – sharp knives are easier to use and are safer as they are less liable to slip.

chopping boards
A selection of chopping boards is essential for the preparation of most ingredients. Use separate boards for preparing raw meat, chicken, fish and vegetables.

frying pans
A few frying pans in different sizes are a boon to the tapas maker. You'll need them for a range of dishes. A heavy-based 25-cm/10-inch frying pan is essential for making tortilla.

deep-fat fryer
This is a useful piece of equipment, although not essential – a deep saucepan or frying pan can be used instead.

griddle pan
This can be flat or ridged and is usually made of cast iron for even heat distribution. It should always be used over a high heat and is ideal for searing pieces of meat, fish and vegetables. The ridged version marks the food attractively with charred lines.

food processor or blender
Although both costly and bulky, this is a very useful piece of kitchen equipment that chops, slices, grinds, beats and blends.

mortar and pestle
These are useful for mashing garlic and for grinding spices if you don't have a food processor.

cazuelas
These traditional earthenware Spanish ovenproof dishes come in a range of sizes, from small individual serving bowls to larger dishes suitable for taking straight from oven to table.

serving platters
In a tapas bar the food is usually served in individual cazuelas. However, when entertaining guests at home, it can be easier to serve some dishes on larger serving platters.

metal skewers
Several of these, large and small, are useful. The smaller ones can be used to cook and serve individual portions of dishes.

cocktail sticks
Wooden cocktail sticks are useful for skewering individual tapas and for securing rolled tapas.

>1>2>3

essential ingredients

> olives
These range from the tiny green *arbequinas* to the larger *manzanillas* and the smooth black *aragón*. Olives are frequently marinated in a spiced oil and manzanillas are often stuffed with anchovies, pimientos and blanched almonds.

> olive oil
This essential ingredient in the Spanish kitchen is used for cooking, preserving and flavouring, depending on its degree of refinement. Regular olive oil is best reserved for cooking and preserving; the more strongly flavoured virgin and extra virgin oils can be used in dressings and marinades.

> almonds
Almonds are used in all types of Spanish dishes, both sweet and savoury. A dish of whole almonds is one of the simplest tapas dishes there is.

> chillies
Fresh and dried chillies make an essential contribution to many Spanish dishes, and are generally used to enhance the flavours of the other ingredients rather than to add heat.

> anchovies
Anchovy fillets packed in oil are used in casseroles and stews as a flavour enhancer or served as a tapa with olives or pickled onions.

> chorizo
The best known of all of Spain's sausages, chorizo is made with pork and paprika. It comes in many varieties, from raw to cured, smoked to unsmoked, and spicy to mildly spiced.

> Serrano ham
Cured, air-dried ham, usually served in very thin slices with bread, or as part of a cured meats platter. The premium variety of Serrano ham is known as *jamón Ibérico* or *pata negra*, named after the black Iberian pig from which it is made.

> *lomo*
This dry-cured pork loin is similar in texture to *cecina* and is used in the same way. The less fat it contains the more expensive it is.

> *salchichon*
This dry-cured, highly spiced sausage is made with pork from the Spanish white pig. It has a slightly nutty flavour and a creamy texture.

> *cecina*
This salt-cured, air-dried beef is a true Spanish delicacy. Although it is cured in salt for up to seven months, it doesn't taste excessively salty.

> Manchego cheese
Used in cooking and eaten with honey as a tapa or dessert, the intensity of the flavour of this salty, tangy sheep's cheese depends on the degree of ageing.

>4>5>6

> ***pimientos del piquillo***
These small red peppers from the Navarre region are usually chargrilled and preserved in olive oil with herbs, a process that enhances their flavour.

> **artichoke hearts**
A jar of artichoke hearts in oil is a good starting point for a range of tapas, deep-fried in a light batter, added to a paella, used as a stuffing for tomatoes or red peppers, or combined with other ingredients, such as Serrano ham and quail's eggs.

> **capers**
The pickled flower buds of the Mediterranean caper bush are used to add zing to a range of dishes.

> **dates**
The Moors can be thanked for the prevalence of dried fruits in the Spanish diet. Dried dates, in particular, are used in both savoury and sweet dishes and will be served as a simple tapa with cheese and honey.

> **pine nuts**
Pine trees are ubiquitous in Spain and the kernels found in the cones are frequently used in the Spanish kitchen, especially in dishes from the Catalan region.

> **paprika**
This red spice comes in several different heats, depending on the variety of red pepper used to make it. It can also be smoked, giving it the earthy flavour that is so characteristic of paella.

> **saffron**
The world's most expensive spice, made from the stigmas of the crocus, was introduced to Spain by the Moors in the eighth century. Spanish saffron is renowned as the best in the world and is an essential ingredient in paella.

> **beans**
Beans of all kinds are used extensively in soups, stews and salads, with the versatile chickpea being especially popular. Dried beans need to be soaked overnight and cooked before use, but the canned varieties are more convenient to use and give equally good results.

> **rice**
A variety of short-grain rice grown in the Middle East is the most suitable rice for making paella. Look for paella rice or Calasparra rice – pudding rice and risotto rice are too soft and creamy for paella, in which the grains of rice should be distinctly separate.

> **herbs**
Fresh and dried herbs are an essential component of Spanish cuisine. Try to keep a supply of coriander, oregano, parsley, thyme and coriander seeds.

> **sherry vinegar**
Made from the must of the sherry grape, this sweetish, complex-flavoured vinegar adds depth to soups, casseroles and dressings. If you cannot find any, use a good balsamic vinegar instead.

small plates

stuffed olives

serves 6

ingredients

4 tbsp Spanish extra virgin olive oil
1 tbsp sherry vinegar, or to taste
2 tbsp very finely chopped parsley
finely grated rind of ½ orange
18 large stoned black olives
18 large stoned green olives
12 anchovy fillets in oil, drained
½ grilled red pepper in oil, drained and cut into 12 small pieces
12 blanched almonds

>1 Whisk together the oil, vinegar, parsley and orange rind in a small serving bowl, adding extra vinegar to taste. Set aside.

>2 Make a lengthways slit in 12 of the black olives and 12 of the green olives without cutting all the way through.

>3 Roll up the anchovy fillets and gently press them into the cavities of six of the slit green olives and six of the slit black olives.

>4 Use the pieces of red pepper to stuff the remaining slit olives.

Slip a blanched almond into the centre of each of the remaining olives.

Add all the olives to the bowl of dressing and stir gently.

Serve with wooden cocktail sticks for spearing the olives.

chillies rellenos

serves 4

ingredients

3 eggs, separated
55 g/2 oz plain flour
325 g/11½ oz Cheddar cheese
16 fresh green jalapeño chillies
sunflower oil or corn oil, for deep-frying

>1 Whisk the egg whites in a dry, grease-free bowl until stiff.

Beat the egg yolks in a separate bowl, then fold in the whites.

>3 Spread out the flour in a shallow dish.

Cut 225 g/8 oz of the cheese into 16 sticks and grate the remainder.

>5 Make a slit in the side of each chilli and scrape out the seeds. Rinse the cavities and pat dry with kitchen paper.

>6 Place a stick of cheese inside each chilli. Preheat the grill. Heat enough oil for deep-frying in a large saucepan or deep-fat fryer to 180–190°C/350–375°F, or until a cube of bread browns in 30 seconds.

>7 Dip the chillies in the egg mixture, then in the flour. Deep-fry, turning occasionally, until golden brown all over. Drain well on kitchen paper.

>8 Arrange the chillies in a baking dish and sprinkle over the grated cheese. Place under the preheated grill until the cheese has melted.

Serve immediately while still hot.

salted almonds

serves 6–8

ingredients
4 tbsp Spanish olive oil
225 g/8 oz whole
  blanched almonds
sea salt
1 tsp Spanish sweet paprika

>1 Preheat the oven to 180°C/350°F/Gas Mark 4. Place the oil in a roasting tin and swirl it around to cover the base. Add the almonds and toss so that they are evenly coated in the oil, then spread them out in a single layer.

>2 Roast the almonds in the preheated oven for 20 minutes, or until they are light golden brown, tossing several times during the cooking.

Serve the almonds warm or cold – they are at their best when served freshly cooked.

>3 Drain the almonds on kitchen paper, then transfer them to a bowl.

While the almonds are still warm, sprinkle with plenty of sea salt and paprika and toss together to coat.

dates with cheese & ham

makes 24

ingredients

24 large ready-to-eat dried dates
140 g/5 oz Manchego cheese
6 thin slices Serrano ham
Spanish olive oil, for brushing

>1 Using a small knife, slit each date and remove the stones, if necessary, then set aside.

>2 Cut away the cheese rind, then cut the cheese into 24 equal-sized pieces that will fit in the dates, each about 5 mm/¼ inch thick.

>3 Push the cheese inside the dates and close the dates around the cheese.

>4 Cut each slice of ham into four long strips.

>5 Wrap a strip of ham around each date and gently press the ham to seal.

>6 Heat a frying pan over a very high heat. Brush the surface with oil, then use kitchen paper to wipe out the excess.

>7 Working in batches, if necessary, add as many stuffed dates as will fit in the pan in a single layer and fry for 1–1½ minutes, until the ham is crisp.

>8 Turn the dates and fry on the other side for a further minute, or until the cheese is soft and the ham is crisp.

Leave to cool for 2 minutes, then serve hot with wooden cocktail sticks for spearing the dates.

prawn & chorizo pinchos

makes 24

ingredients

½ lemon, sliced
1 tbsp sea salt
24 large peeled, raw prawns, thawed if frozen
140 g/5 oz chorizo
24 fresh basil leaves
lemon wedges, to serve

>1 Bring a large saucepan of water to the boil with the lemon slices and salt.

>2 Cut along the length of each prawn and remove and discard the dark vein. Set aside.

>3 Remove and discard the casing from the chorizo, then cut it into 24 x 5-mm/¼-inch slices and set aside.

>4 Add the prawns to the boiling water, reduce the heat to low and simmer for 1½–2 minutes, until the prawns turn pink and begin to curl.

>5 Drain the prawns, then place under cold running water to stop the cooking. Pat dry with a clean tea towel.

>6 Use a wooden cocktail stick to skewer a piece of chorizo, a basil leaf and then a prawn. Cover and chill until required.

Arrange on a serving plate and serve with lemon wedges for squeezing over.

tomato bread

serves 2–4

ingredients

4 slices of bread from a long, thin loaf, cut diagonally
2 ripe tomatoes, halved
1 garlic clove, finely chopped
2 tbsp Spanish olive oil

>1 If the bread is soft, toast it under a preheated grill until light golden on both sides.

>2 Rub one side of each slice of bread with half a tomato.

Serve immediately, before the bread has time to become soggy.

>3 Sprinkle over the chopped garlic.

>4 Drizzle the oil over the top.

hot anchovy dip with vegetables

serves 8

ingredients

100 g/3½ oz anchovy fillets in oil
4 large garlic cloves, unpeeled
sea salt
125 ml/4 fl oz Spanish extra virgin olive oil, plus extra if needed
sherry vinegar, to taste
pepper
selection of freshly prepared vegetables, such as chicory leaves, courgette slices and red pepper strips, to serve

>1 Drain the anchovy fillets, reserving the oil.

>2 Finely chop the anchovies and transfer them with the reserved oil to a frying pan over a low heat.

>3 Put the garlic cloves on a chopping board and bash with the side of a large cook's knife. Remove and discard the skins.

>4 Very lightly sprinkle the garlic with salt and use the flat of the knife to crush the garlic into a paste.

>5 Add the garlic paste and olive oil to the pan, increase the heat to medium-high and stir until the anchovies dissolve. Make sure that the garlic does not burn.

>6 Add vinegar and pepper to taste.

Transfer to a serving dish and serve hot with a selection of freshly prepared vegetables for dipping.

russian salad

makes 16–20

ingredients

2 eggs
350 g/12 oz new potatoes, scrubbed
125 g/4½ oz carrots, peeled and diced
125 g/4½ oz shelled fresh peas or thawed frozen peas
4 spring onions, finely chopped
125 ml/4 fl oz mayonnaise
1 tbsp chopped fresh dill
1 tsp Spanish sweet paprika, or to taste
16–20 slices of bread from a long, thin loaf
salt and pepper

>1 Place the eggs in a saucepan and pour in enough water to cover by 2.5 cm/1 inch. Bring to the boil, then reduce the heat to low and simmer for 9 minutes.

>2 Drain the eggs and place under cold running water until cool enough to handle.

>3 Shell the eggs and finely chop the yolks and whites, then set aside.

>4 Meanwhile, bring a saucepan of lightly salted water to the boil and add the potatoes. Bring back to the boil and cook for 15–20 minutes, until tender.

>5 Use a slotted spoon to remove the potatoes from the water and place under cold running water until cool enough to handle. Peel and cut into 5-mm/¼-inch dice, then set aside.

>6 Add the carrots to the potato water, bring back to the boil and cook for 2 minutes. Add the peas and cook for a further 5 minutes if fresh, or 3 minutes if thawed, until the vegetables are tender. Drain well and leave to cool.

>7 Beat the spring onions, mayonnaise, dill and paprika in a large bowl.

>8 Add the vegetables and eggs and gently mix together. Season to taste with salt and pepper.

Mound the vegetable mixture on the bread slices. Eat within 30 minutes, before the bread has time to become soggy.

cured meat platter with herb salad

serves 8

ingredients

4 ripe figs
125 g/4½ oz chorizo
125 g/4½ oz thinly sliced Iberico ham
125 g/4½ oz thinly sliced Serrano ham
125 g/4½ oz thinly sliced lomo
125 g/4½ oz thinly sliced salchichon
125 g/4½ oz thinly sliced cecina
3 tbsp extra virgin olive oil, plus extra to serve
2 tsp moscatel
6 tbsp fresh flat-leaf parsley leaves
1 tbsp fresh mint leaves
1 tbsp snipped fresh chives
salt and pepper
country-style bread, to serve

>1 Cut each fig into quarters lengthways. Arrange on one side of a large serving platter.

>2 Remove and discard the casing from the chorizo. Thinly slice the chorizo, then transfer to the platter.

Serve with plenty of bread, and extra oil for dipping.

>3 Arrange the remaining meats on the platter, keeping each variety separate.

>4 Put the oil and moscatel into a bowl and season to taste with salt and pepper, then whisk until blended. Add the herbs and quickly toss together. Immediately transfer to the platter with the meats.

fried manchego cheese

makes 6

ingredients

200 g/7 oz Manchego cheese
3 tbsp plain flour
1 egg
1 tsp water
85 g/3 oz fresh white or brown breadcrumbs
sunflower oil, for deep-frying
salt and pepper

>1 Cut the cheese into six triangles, each about 1 cm/½ inch thick.

>2 Place the flour in a polythene bag and season to taste with salt and pepper.

>3 Break the egg into a shallow dish, add the water and beat together.

>4 Spread out the breadcrumbs on a large plate.

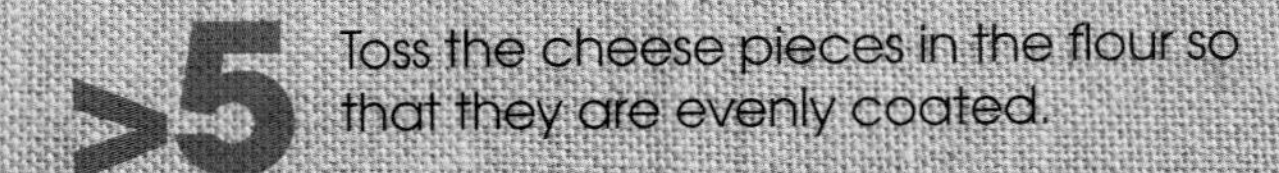

>5 Toss the cheese pieces in the flour so that they are evenly coated.

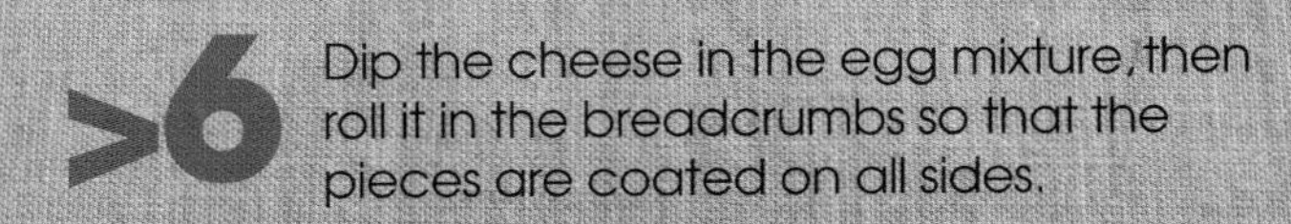

>6 Dip the cheese in the egg mixture, then roll it in the breadcrumbs so that the pieces are coated on all sides.

>7 Heat enough oil for deep-frying in a large, heavy-based frying pan or deep-fat fryer to 180–190°C/350–375°F, or until a cube of bread browns in 30 seconds. Add the cheese and fry for 1–2 minutes, until golden brown.

>8 Using a slotted spoon, remove the fried cheese and drain well on kitchen paper.

Serve immediately.

chorizo-stuffed mushrooms

makes 24

ingredients

24 chestnut mushrooms, each about 4 cm/ 1½ inches in diameter
140 g/5 oz chorizo
1 tbsp Spanish olive oil, plus extra for brushing
6 spring onions, very finely chopped
¼ tsp Spanish sweet paprika
80 g/2¾ oz fine dry white breadcrumbs
finely grated rind of 1 lemon
2 tbsp very finely chopped fresh parsley
salt and pepper

>1 Preheat the oven to 180°C/350°F/Gas Mark 4. Brush a shallow roasting tin with oil. Remove the stalks from the mushrooms and finely chop, then set aside.

>2 Lightly brush the mushrooms with oil. Lightly season the inside of the mushrooms with salt and pepper and set aside.

>3 Remove and discard the casing from the chorizo, then finely chop.

>4 Add the chorizo to a dry frying pan over a medium–high heat and fry, using a wooden spoon to break it up, for 3–5 minutes, until it gives off its fat. Transfer to a bowl using a slotted spoon, leaving as much fat as possible in the pan.

>5 Add the oil to the pan, then add the spring onions, paprika and chopped mushroom stalks and season to taste with salt and pepper. Fry, stirring, for 3–5 minutes, until the onions are soft.

>6 Add the onion mixture to the chorizo and stir in the breadcrumbs, lemon rind and parsley. Adjust the seasoning, adding salt and pepper if needed.

>7 Use a teaspoon to divide the mixture between the mushrooms, mounding it slightly. Arrange the mushrooms in a single layer in the prepared tin.

>8 Bake in the preheated oven for 15 minutes, until tender. Carefully transfer the mushrooms to kitchen paper to drain. Leave to stand for 5 minutes.

Transfer the mushrooms to a serving platter and serve hot, warm or at room temperature.

seafood salad

makes 16–20

ingredients

125 g/4½ oz drained canned small prawns
125 g/4½ oz drained canned white crabmeat
1 celery stick, very finely chopped
1 small red onion, very finely chopped
6 tbsp mayonnaise
lemon juice, to taste
2 tbsp finely chopped fresh parsley
16–20 slices of bread from a long, thin loaf
Spanish sweet paprika, for dusting
salt and pepper
32–40 thin, short strips grilled red pepper in oil, drained, to garnish

>1 Put the prawns and crabmeat into a bowl and stir together.

>2 Add the celery, onion, mayonnaise and lemon juice and stir together.

Arrange on a serving platter and garnish each with two slices of red pepper arranged to form an 'X'. Eat within 30 minutes, before the bread has time to become soggy.

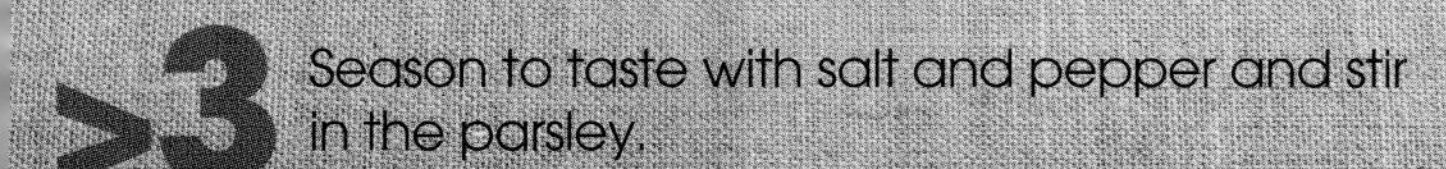

>3 Season to taste with salt and pepper and stir in the parsley.

>4 Mound the vegetable mixture on the bread slices and lightly dust with paprika.

tapenade

makes about 500 ml/18 fl oz

ingredients

100 g/3½ oz canned anchovy fillets in oil
350 g/12 oz black olives, stoned and roughly chopped
2 garlic cloves, roughly chopped
2 tbsp capers, drained and rinsed
1 tbsp Dijon mustard
3 tbsp Spanish extra virgin olive oil
2 tbsp lemon juice
slices of crusty bread, to serve

>1 Drain the anchovies, reserving the oil from the can.

>2 Roughly chop the anchovies.

>3 Place the anchovies in a food processor or blender.

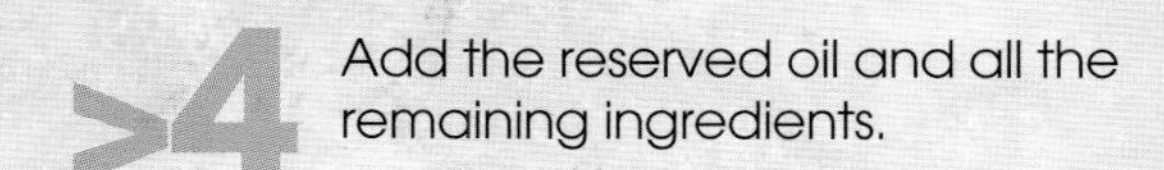

>4 Add the reserved oil and all the remaining ingredients.

>5 Process to a smooth purée. Stop and scrape down the sides if necessary.

>6 Transfer the tapenade to a dish, cover with clingfilm and chill in the refrigerator until required.

Bring to room temperature, remove the clingfilm and serve spread on slices of bread.

romesco sauce

makes about 300 ml/10 fl oz

ingredients

4 large, ripe tomatoes
16 blanched almonds
3 large garlic cloves, unpeeled
1 dried sweet chilli, such as ñora, soaked in water for 20 minutes and patted dry
4 dried red chillies, soaked in water for 20 minutes and patted dry
pinch of sugar
150 ml/5 fl oz Spanish extra virgin olive oil
1½ tbsp sherry vinegar, or to taste
salt and pepper

>1 Preheat the oven to 180°C/350°F/Gas Mark 4. Put the tomatoes, almonds and garlic in a roasting tin and roast in the preheated oven for 20 minutes. Check the almonds after about 7 minutes because they can burn quickly; remove from the oven as soon as they are golden.

>2 Peel the roasted garlic and tomatoes, then put them into a food processor with the soaked sweet chilli and red chillies and process until finely chopped.

>3 Add the almonds and sugar and process again.

>4 With the motor running, slowly add the oil through the feed tube.

>5 Add the vinegar and process briefly. Add extra vinegar and salt and pepper to taste.

>6 Leave to stand for at least 2 hours, or cover and chill for up to 3 days.

Bring to room temperature and stir in any oil that has separated. Serve as an accompaniment to a range of tapas dishes.

aïoli

makes about 350 ml/12 fl oz

ingredients
3–4 large garlic cloves, or to taste
pinch of sea salt
2 large egg yolks
1 tsp lemon juice
300 ml/10 fl oz Spanish extra virgin olive oil
salt and pepper

>1 Put the garlic cloves into a mortar with the sea salt and mash to a paste with a pestle.

>2 Put the paste in a food processor, add the egg yolks and lemon juice and process.

Bring to room temperature before serving as an accompaniment to a range of tapas dishes.

>3 With the motor still running, slowly dribble in the oil through the feed tube until an emulsion forms and the sauce thickens.

>4 Taste and adjust the seasoning, adding salt and pepper if needed. Serve immediately, or cover and chill for up to 3 days.

vegetarian

spanish tortilla

serves 6–8

ingredients

125 ml/4 fl oz Spanish olive oil

600 g/1 lb 5 oz potatoes, peeled and thinly sliced

1 large onion, thinly sliced

6 large eggs

salt and pepper

>1 Heat the oil in a 25-cm/10-inch frying pan over a high heat. Reduce the heat, then add the potatoes and onion and cook for 15–20 minutes, or until the potatoes are tender.

>2 Beat the eggs in a large bowl and generously season with salt and pepper.

>3 Drain the potatoes and onion through a colander, reserving the oil. Very gently stir the potatoes and onion into the eggs, then leave to stand for 10 minutes.

>4 Add 4 tablespoons of the reserved oil to the frying pan and heat over a medium heat.

>5 Add the egg mixture and smooth the surface, pressing the potatoes and onions into an even layer. Cook for 5 minutes, shaking the pan occasionally, until the base is set.

>6 Use a spatula to loosen the side of the tortilla. Place a large plate over the top and carefully invert the pan and plate together so the tortilla drops on to the plate.

>7 Add 1 tablespoon of the remaining reserved oil to the pan. Carefully slide the tortilla back into the pan, cooked side up.

>8 Continue cooking for 3 minutes, or until the eggs are set and the base is golden brown.

Slide the tortilla on to a plate. Leave to stand for at least 5 minutes before cutting into wedges.

patatas bravas

serves 6

ingredients

2 tbsp Spanish olive oil, plus extra for shallow-frying
1 onion, finely chopped
2 garlic cloves, sliced
3½ tbsp vegetarian white wine or dry Spanish sherry
400 g/14 oz canned chopped tomatoes
2 tsp white or red wine vinegar
1–2 tsp dried chilli flakes
2 tsp Spanish hot or sweet smoked paprika
1 kg/2 lb 4 oz potatoes, washed but not peeled and cut into chunks

>1 Heat the 2 tablespoons of oil in a large saucepan, add the onion and cook over a medium heat, stirring occasionally, for 5 minutes, or until softened. Add the garlic and cook, stirring, for 30 seconds.

>2 Add the wine and bring to the boil. Add the tomatoes, vinegar, chilli flakes and paprika, reduce the heat and simmer, uncovered, for 10–15 minutes, until a thick sauce forms.

>3 Using a hand-held blender, blend the sauce in the pan until smooth. Set aside.

>4 In a large frying pan, heat enough oil to come about 2.5 cm/1 inch up the side of the pan. Add the potatoes and cook over a medium–high heat, turning occasionally, for 10–15 minutes, until golden brown.

>5 Remove with a slotted spoon and drain on kitchen paper.

>6 Meanwhile, gently reheat the sauce.

Transfer the potatoes to a warmed serving dish and drizzle over the sauce. Serve immediately.

sautéed garlic mushrooms

serves 6

ingredients
450 g/1 lb button mushrooms
5 tbsp Spanish olive oil
2 garlic cloves, finely chopped
lemon juice, to taste
4 tbsp chopped fresh parsley
salt and pepper
lemon wedges, to garnish
country-style bread, to serve

>1 Halve or quarter any large mushrooms.

>2 Heat the oil in a large frying pan. Add the garlic and fry for 30 seconds–1 minute, or until lightly browned.

Transfer to a warmed serving dish and garnish with lemon wedges. Serve with bread to mop up the juices.

>3 Add the mushrooms and sauté over a high heat, stirring frequently, until they have absorbed the oil. Reduce the heat to low. When the juices have come out of the mushrooms, increase the heat and sauté for 4–5 minutes, stirring frequently, until the juices have almost evaporated.

>4 Add a squeeze of lemon juice and season to taste with salt and pepper. Stir in the parsley and cook for a further minute.

chargrilled vegetable platter

serves 8

ingredients

125 ml/4 fl oz Spanish olive oil
4 garlic cloves, roughly chopped
4 fresh thyme sprigs
1.5 kg/3 lb 5 oz fresh vegetables, such as asparagus, aubergines, courgettes, fennel, thick spring onions and red peppers
salt and pepper
romesco sauce (see page 60), to serve

>1 Put the oil, garlic and thyme into a bowl and set aside to infuse for at least 1 hour.

>2 Hold each asparagus spear at each end and bend until the woody stalk snaps. Discard the broken ends. If the stalks are thick, cut them in half lengthways.

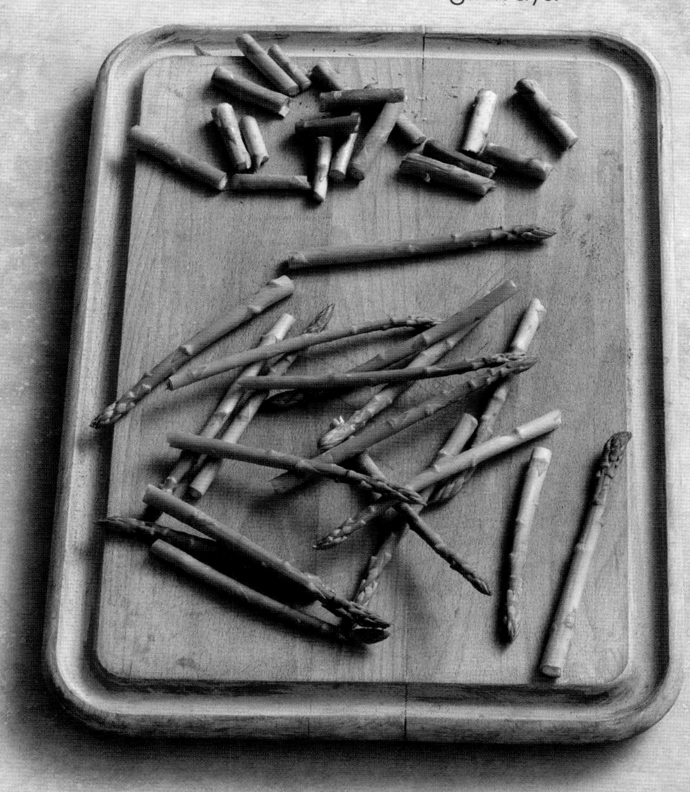

>3 Trim the aubergines and courgettes and cut them lengthways into 5-mm/¼-inch slices.

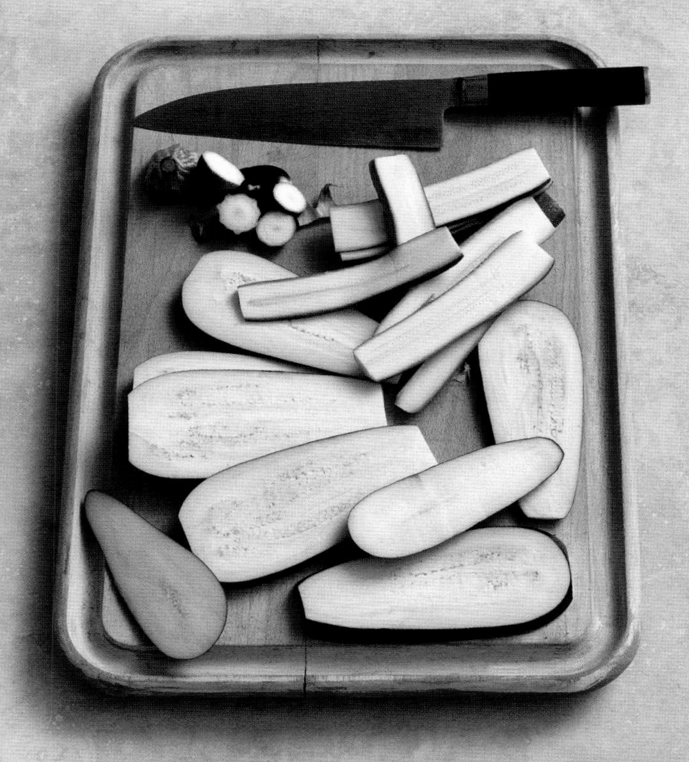

>4 Trim the fennel and slice crossways through the bulb. Trim the spring onions.

>5 Quarter, core and deseed the red pepper.

>6 Heat a ridged, cast-iron griddle pan over a high heat until very hot. Brush with a little of the garlic-infused oil.

>7 Working in batches, add the vegetables to the pan, placing the red pepper pieces skin side down. Sprinkle with salt and pepper and cook until they start to become tender.

>8 Using tongs, turn the vegetables over and continue cooking until tender. Continue until all the vegetables are cooked, brushing the pan with oil as needed.

Transfer the vegetables to a warmed platter as they are cooked and serve hot, warm or at room temperature with romesco sauce.

courgette fritters with pine nut sauce

serves 6–8

ingredients

3 tbsp plain flour
1 tsp paprika
1 large egg
2 tbsp milk
450 g/1 lb baby courgettes, cut diagonally into 5-mm/¼-inch slices
sunflower oil, for shallow-frying
sea salt, for sprinkling

pine nut sauce

100 g/3½ oz pine nuts
1 garlic clove, peeled
3 tbsp Spanish extra virgin olive oil
1 tbsp lemon juice
3 tbsp water
1 tbsp chopped fresh flat-leaf parsley
salt and pepper

>1 To make the sauce, put the pine nuts and garlic into a food processor and process to form a purée. With the motor still running, gradually add the olive oil, lemon juice and water to form a smooth sauce.

>2 Stir in the parsley and season to taste with salt and pepper. Transfer to a serving bowl and set aside.

>3 Put the flour and paprika into a polythene bag and shake well.

>4 Beat together the egg and milk in a large bowl.

>5 Add the courgette slices to the flour mixture and toss until coated. Shake off the excess flour.

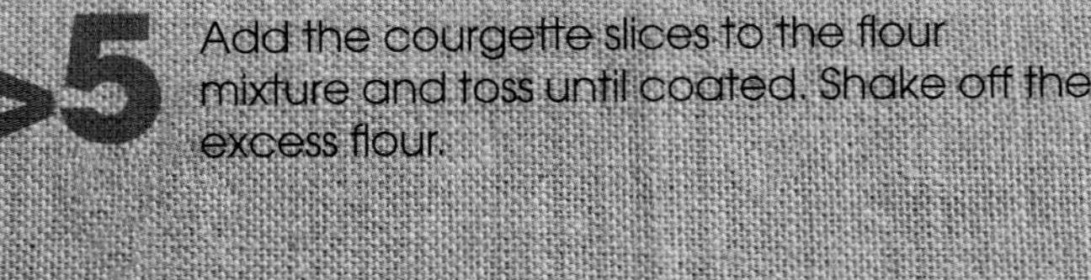

>6 In a large frying pan, heat enough sunflower oil to come about 1 cm/½ inch up the side of the pan. Dip the courgette slices, one at a time, into the egg mixture, then put them into the hot oil.

>7 Fry the courgette slices, in batches and in a single layer so that they do not overcrowd the pan, for 2 minutes, or until they are crisp and golden brown.

>8 Using a slotted spoon, remove the fritters from the pan and drain on kitchen paper. Continue until all the courgette slices are cooked.

Transfer the fritters to a serving platter. Sprinkle with a little sea salt, drizzle over the pine nut sauce and serve piping hot.

stewed chickpeas

serves 8

ingredients

6 tbsp Spanish olive oil
1 large onion, finely chopped
800 g/1 lb 12 oz canned chopped tomatoes
4 large garlic cloves, chopped
800 g/1 lb 12 oz canned chickpeas, drained and rinsed
1 tsp Spanish sweet paprika, or to taste
salt and pepper
sliced country-style bread, to serve

>1 Heat the oil in a large saucepan over a medium heat. Add the onion, reduce the heat to low and fry, stirring, for 5–8 minutes, until soft.

>2 Add the tomatoes and garlic and simmer for 10 minutes, stirring occasionally.

Spoon into a serving bowl and serve hot or at room temperature with bread.

>3 Stir in the chickpeas and paprika and season to taste with salt and pepper. Cover the pan and bring to the boil.

>4 Reduce the heat to low and simmer, partially covered, for 15 minutes, until the chickpeas are coated in a thick sauce. Adjust the seasoning, adding salt and pepper if needed.

flamenco eggs

serves 4

ingredients

4 tbsp Spanish olive oil
1 onion, thinly sliced
2 garlic cloves, finely chopped
2 small red peppers, deseeded and chopped
4 tomatoes, peeled, deseeded and chopped
1 tbsp chopped fresh parsley
200 g/7 oz canned sweetcorn kernels, drained
4 eggs
salt and cayenne pepper

>1 Preheat the oven to 180°C/350°F/Gas Mark 4. Heat the oil in a large, heavy-based frying pan. Add the onion and garlic and cook over a low heat, stirring occasionally, for 5 minutes, or until soft.

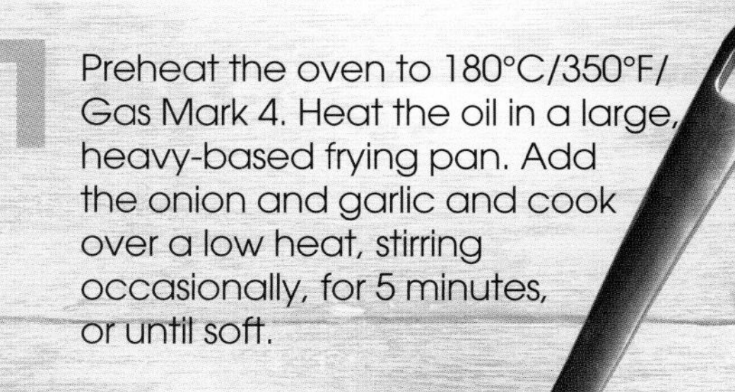

>2 Add the red peppers and cook, stirring occasionally, for a further 10 minutes.

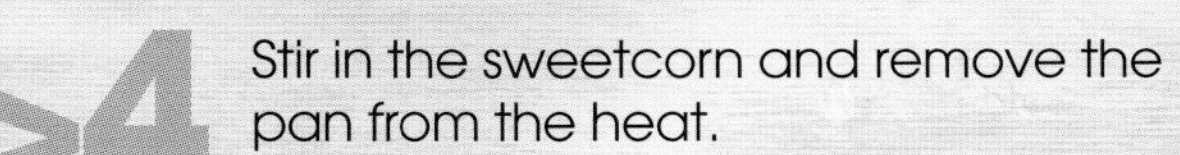

>3 Stir in the tomatoes and parsley, season to taste with salt and cayenne pepper and cook for a further 5 minutes.

>4 Stir in the sweetcorn and remove the pan from the heat.

>5 Divide the mixture between four individual baking dishes. Use the back of a spoon to make a hollow in the centre of each portion using the back of a spoon.

>6 Break an egg into each hollow. Bake in the preheated oven for 15–25 minutes, or until the eggs have set.

Serve the eggs hot and eat straight from the baking dishes.

roasted pepper salad

serves 8

ingredients

3 red peppers
3 yellow peppers
5 tbsp Spanish extra virgin olive oil, plus extra for brushing
2 tbsp sherry vinegar
2 garlic cloves, chopped
pinch of sugar
1 tbsp capers, drained and rinsed
8 small black Spanish olives
2 tbsp chopped fresh marjoram, plus extra sprigs to garnish
salt and pepper

>1 Preheat the oven to 200°C/400°F/Gas Mark 6. Brush the peppers with oil and put in a roasting tin. Roast in the preheated oven for 30 minutes, then turn over and roast for a further 10 minutes, until the skins have blistered and blackened.

>2 Using a slotted spoon, transfer the roasted peppers to a polythene bag and leave for 15 minutes, or until cool enough to handle.

>3 Holding the peppers one at a time over a clean bowl, use a sharp knife to make a small hole in the base, then gently squeeze out the juices and set aside.

>4 Peel, core and deseed the peppers, then cut them into neat, thin strips and arrange them attractively on a serving platter.

Add the oil, vinegar, garlic, sugar, and salt and pepper to taste to the reserved pepper juices. Whisk together until combined, then drizzle over the peppers.

>6 Sprinkle over the capers, olives and chopped marjoram.

Garnish with marjoram sprigs and serve at room temperature.

catalan spinach

serves 8

ingredients
4 tbsp raisins
900 g/2 lb spinach, rinsed
2 tbsp Spanish olive oil
1 large garlic clove, chopped
2 tbsp pine nuts
pinch of dried chilli flakes, or to taste
salt and pepper

>1 Soak the raisins in lukewarm water for 15 minutes. Drain well and set aside.

>2 Meanwhile, put the spinach into a large saucepan with just the water clinging to the leaves. Turn the heat to high and stir for 3–5 minutes, until the spinach is very tender. Drain well. When cool enough to handle, squeeze out any excess water, then finely chop.

Spoon the spinach into cazuelas and serve immediately.

>3 Heat the oil in a large frying pan over a medium heat. Add the garlic and fry, stirring, for 1–2 minutes, until golden. Stir in the raisins, pine nuts and chilli flakes and stir for 2 minutes, until the pine nuts are toasted.

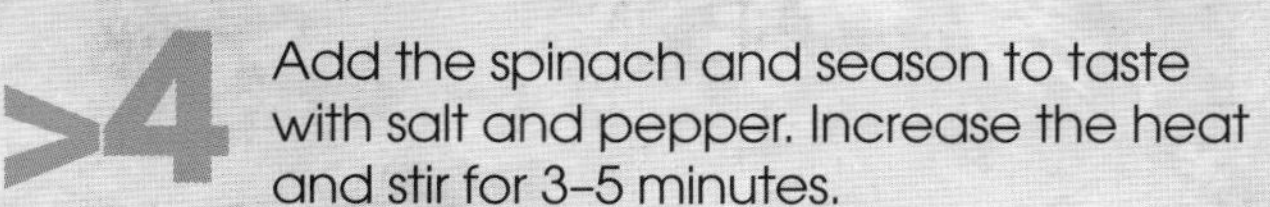

>4 Add the spinach and season to taste with salt and pepper. Increase the heat and stir for 3–5 minutes.

pisto manchego

serves 8

ingredients

4 large tomatoes
1 red onion
1 aubergine, about 500 g/1 lb 2 oz
1 courgette
4 garlic cloves, peeled
2 green peppers
2 red peppers
125 ml/4 fl oz Spanish olive oil
2–3 tsp sherry vinegar, to taste
salt and pepper
crusty bread, to serve

>1 Cut a 'X' in the stem end of each tomato. Put the tomatoes into a large heatproof bowl and pour over enough boiling water to cover. Leave to stand for 30 seconds, or until the skins split.

>2 Drain the tomatoes and immediately rinse under cold running water to cool. Use a small knife to peel off the skins.

>3 Cut the tomatoes in half and use a teaspoon to scoop out the seeds and cores. Finely dice the flesh.

>4 Peel the onion. Trim the aubergine and courgette. Finely chop the onion, aubergine, courgette and garlic.

>5 Core, deseed and finely dice the peppers.

>6 Heat the oil in a large frying pan over a medium heat. Add the onion and peppers and fry, stirring occasionally, for 8–10 minutes.

>7 Stir in the garlic, tomatoes, aubergine and courgette. Bring to the boil, stirring, then reduce the heat and simmer for 15–20 minutes.

>8 Season to taste with salt and pepper, then stir in the vinegar.

Transfer the vegetable mixture to a serving bowl and serve hot or at room temperature with bread.

devilled eggs

makes 16

ingredients

8 large eggs
2 whole canned or bottled pimientos del piquillo
16 stoned green Spanish olives
5 tbsp mayonnaise
8 drops of hot pepper sauce
large pinch of cayenne pepper
salt and pepper
Little Gem lettuce leaves, to serve
Spanish paprika, to garnish

>1 Put the eggs into a saucepan, cover with cold water and slowly bring to the boil. Reduce the heat to very low, cover and simmer gently for 10 minutes. Drain the eggs and place under cold running water until they are cold.

>2 Crack the eggshells and remove. Halve the eggs lengthways, then carefully remove the yolks.

>3 Place the yolks in a sieve set over a bowl and rub through, then mash with a fork.

>4 Place the pimientos on kitchen paper to dry well, then finely chop, reserving 16 small strips.

>5 Finely chop half the olives. Halve the remaining olives.

>6 Add the chopped pimientos and chopped olives to the mashed egg yolks. Add the mayonnaise, mix together well, then add the hot pepper sauce, cayenne pepper, and salt and pepper to taste.

>7 Use a teaspoon to spoon a little of the egg yolk mixture into the hollow in each egg white half.

>8 Add a small strip of the reserved pimientos and an olive half to the top of each stuffed egg.

Line a platter with lettuce leaves and arrange the eggs on top. Dust with a little paprika and serve.

white bean & pepper salad

serves 8

ingredients

2 large grilled red peppers in oil, drained and oil reserved
800 g/1 lb 12 oz canned haricot beans, butter beans or cannellini beans, drained and rinsed
2 spring onions, finely chopped
2 tbsp capers, drained and rinsed
2 tbsp sherry vinegar, or to taste
Spanish extra virgin olive oil, to taste
salt and pepper
sliced crusty bread, to serve

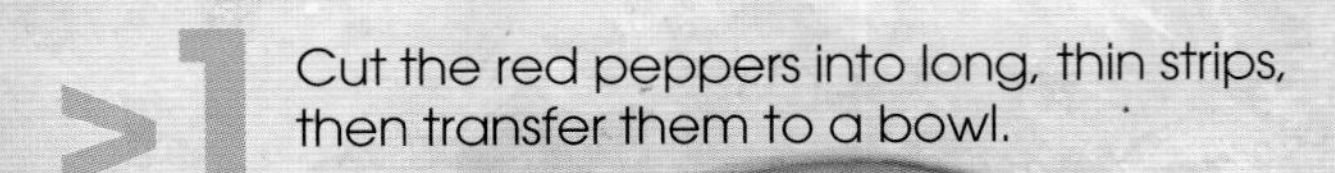

>1 Cut the red peppers into long, thin strips, then transfer them to a bowl.

>2 Add the beans, spring onions and capers and gently mix together.

Spoon the salad into cazuelas and serve immediately or chill until required. Serve with plenty of bread.

>3 Put 4 tablespoons of the reserved oil from the peppers and the vinegar into a bowl and season to taste with salt and pepper. Whisk until blended, then add extra vinegar or oil to taste.

>4 Pour the dressing over the bean mixture and gently mix together.

artichoke & red pepper tortilla

serves 6–8

ingredients

1 large onion, thinly sliced
9 large eggs
250 g/9 oz drained artichoke hearts in oil, quartered and 2 tbsp oil reserved
175 g/6 oz drained grilled red peppers in oil, chopped and 2 tbsp oil reserved
Spanish olive oil, for frying
salt and pepper

>1 Heat the reserved oil from the artichokes and peppers in a 25-cm/10-inch frying pan over a high heat. Reduce the heat, add the onion and fry, stirring, for 8–10 minutes, until golden.

>2 Beat the eggs in a large bowl. Stir in the artichoke hearts and red peppers and season to taste with salt and pepper.

>3 Using a slotted spoon, transfer the onions to the bowl, leaving as much oil in the pan as possible.

>4 Add enough olive oil to the pan to make it up to 4 tablespoons. Heat over a high heat, swirling so it coats the side of the pan.

>5 Add the egg mixture and smooth the surface. Cook for 30 seconds, then reduce the heat to medium and cook for a further 5–7 minutes, shaking the pan occasionally, until the base is set.

>6 Use a spatula to loosen the side of the tortilla.

>7 Place a large plate over the top of the pan. Invert the pan and plate together so the tortilla drops on to the plate.

>8 Add 1 tablespoon of olive oil to the pan and heat. Slide the tortilla into the pan, cooked side up. Continue cooking for 3–5 minutes, until the eggs are set and the base is golden brown.

Slide the tortilla on to a plate. Cut into wedges and serve hot, warm or at room temperature.

broad bean & mushroom salad

serves 8

ingredients

1 red onion
3 tbsp Spanish olive oil, plus extra to serve
900 g/2 lb chestnut mushrooms, sliced
500 g/1 lb 2 oz frozen broad beans
2 tbsp chopped fresh dill
sherry vinegar, to taste
salt and pepper
escarole leaves and sliced crusty bread, to serve

>1 Peel the onion, then cut into quarters and thinly slice. Sprinkle with salt and leave to soften.

>2 Heat the oil in a large frying pan over a high heat.

>3 Add the mushrooms to the pan, season with salt and pepper and fry, stirring frequently, until they have absorbed the oil. Reduce the heat to low. When the juices have come out of the mushrooms, increase the heat and sauté for 4–5 minutes, stirring frequently, until the juices have almost evaporated.

>4 Tip the mushrooms and any remaining liquid into a bowl.

>5 Meanwhile, bring a saucepan of lightly salted water to the boil. Add the broad beans, bring back to the boil and cook for 4–5 minutes, until tender. Drain and immediately transfer to a bowl of iced water.

>6 When the beans are cool enough to handle, drain and use your fingers to pop the beans out of their skins and add to the mushrooms. Leave to cool.

>7 Rinse the onion, then pat dry with kitchen paper.

>8 Add the onion and dill to the mushrooms and beans. Add a splash of vinegar and salt and pepper to taste.

Transfer to a platter lined with escarole leaves and serve with extra oil and slices of bread.

gazpacho

serves 4–6

ingredients

500 g/1 lb 2 oz large, ripe tomatoes, peeled, deseeded and chopped
3 large red peppers, deseeded and chopped
2 tbsp sherry vinegar, or to taste
4 tbsp Spanish olive oil
salt and pepper

to serve

4–6 ice cubes
finely chopped mixed peppers, cucumber and hard-boiled eggs

>1 Put the tomatoes, red peppers, vinegar and oil into a food processor.

>2 Process until blended and the mixture is as smooth or chunky as you like.

To serve, put a selection of garnishes, such as finely chopped peppers, cucumber and hard-boiled eggs, in bowls and let everyone add their own.

>3 Cover and chill for at least 4 hours before serving.

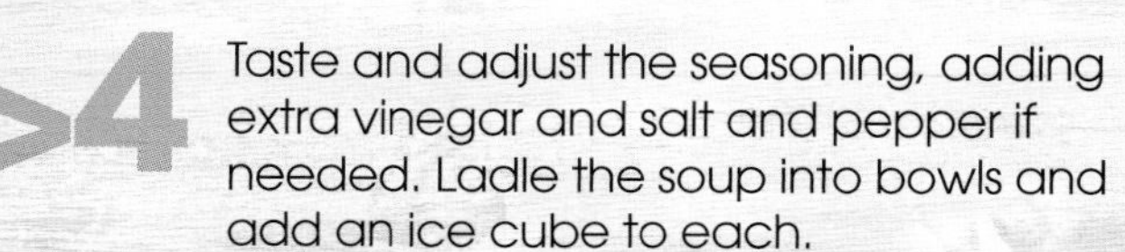

>4 Taste and adjust the seasoning, adding extra vinegar and salt and pepper if needed. Ladle the soup into bowls and add an ice cube to each.

fish & seafood

deep-fried whitebait

serves 4

ingredients

450 g/1 lb fresh whitebait
100 g/3½ oz plain flour
50 g/1¾ oz cornflour
½ tsp salt
200 ml/7 fl oz cold water
1 egg
a few ice cubes
vegetable oil, for deep-frying
aïoli, to serve (see page 64)

>1 Rinse the whitebait and pat dry. Place on kitchen paper and set aside until needed.

>2 Sift together the flour, cornflour and salt into a shallow dish.

>3 Whisk together the water, egg and ice cubes in a jug, then pour onto the flour mixture. Whisk briefly until the mixture is runny, but still lumpy with dry bits of flour still apparent.

>4 Meanwhile, heat enough oil for deep-frying in a large saucepan or deep-fat fryer to 180–190°C/350–375°F, or until a cube of bread browns in 30 seconds.

>5 Dip the whitebait, a few at a time, into the batter and carefully drop into the hot oil.

>6 Deep-fry for 1 minute, until the batter is crisp but not brown. Drain on kitchen paper and keep warm while you cook the remaining whitebait.

Serve the whitebait hot with aïoli.

tuna with pimiento-stuffed olives

serves 4

ingredients

- 2 fresh tuna steaks, weighing about 250 g/9 oz in total and about 2.5 cm/1 inch thick
- 5 tbsp Spanish extra virgin olive oil
- 3 tbsp red wine vinegar
- bunch of fresh thyme sprigs
- 1 bay leaf
- 2 tbsp plain flour
- 1 onion, finely chopped
- 2 garlic cloves, finely chopped
- 85 g/3 oz pimiento-stuffed green olives, halved
- salt and pepper

>1 Cut the tuna steaks in half.

>2 Cut each half into 1 cm/½ inch thick slices against the grain.

>3 Put 3 tablespoons of the oil and all the vinegar into a shallow, non-metallic dish. Strip the leaves from half the thyme sprigs and add to the dish with the bay leaf. Season to taste with salt and pepper.

>4 Add the tuna strips to the dish, turning to coat. Leave to marinate in the refrigerator for 8 hours or overnight.

>5 Put the flour into a polythene bag. Remove the tuna strips from the marinade, reserving the marinade, and add them to the flour. Toss well until lightly coated.

>6 Heat the remaining oil in a large frying pan. Add the onion and garlic and gently fry for 5–10 minutes, or until soft and golden brown.

>7 Add the tuna strips to the pan and fry for 2–5 minutes, turning several times, until the fish becomes opaque.

>8 Add the reserved marinade and the olives to the pan. Bring to the boil and cook for a further 1–2 minutes, stirring, until the fish is tender and the sauce has thickened.

Serve piping hot, garnished with the remaining thyme sprigs.

sizzling chilli prawns

serves 6

ingredients
500 g/1 lb 2 oz large raw prawns
6 tbsp Spanish olive oil
2 garlic cloves, finely chopped
1 small fresh red chilli, deseeded and finely chopped
pinch of paprika
pinch of salt
crusty bread, to serve

>1 Peel the prawns, removing the heads but leaving the tails intact. Cut along the length of each prawn and remove and discard the dark vein.

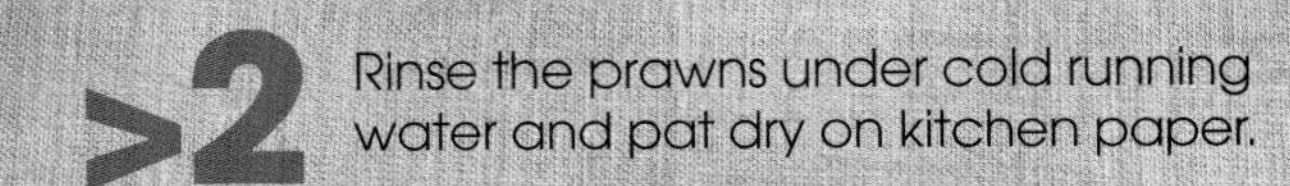

>2 Rinse the prawns under cold running water and pat dry on kitchen paper.

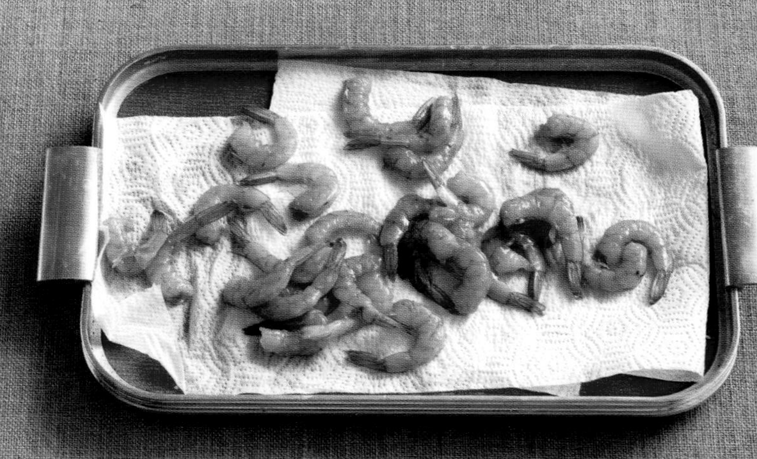

Transfer to a serving dish and serve with bread to mop up the juices.

>3 Heat the oil in a large frying pan until quite hot, then add the garlic and fry for 30 seconds.

>4 Add the prawns, chilli, paprika and salt and fry for 2–3 minutes, stirring constantly, until the prawns turn pink and begin to curl.

monkfish bites with mojo verde sauce

serves 8

ingredients

900 g/2 lb skinless, boneless monkfish fillets
2 tbsp Spanish olive oil

mojo verde sauce

1 large garlic clove, chopped
1 fresh green chilli, deseeded and chopped
1 green pepper, deseeded and chopped
30 g/1 oz fresh coriander leaves
125 ml/4 fl oz Spanish extra virgin olive oil
1 tbsp sherry vinegar, or to taste
salt and pepper

>1 To make the sauce, put the garlic, chilli, green pepper and coriander into a food processor and blend until a paste forms.

>2 Add the extra virgin olive oil and vinegar and blend until smooth. Season to taste with salt and pepper. Chill for up to 1 hour.

>3 Using a small knife, remove the thin, grey membrane from the monkfish.

>4 Cut the monkfish into bite-sized pieces.

>5 Heat the olive oil in a large frying pan over a medium heat. Working in batches, fry the monkfish pieces, turning once, for 3–5 minutes, until just cooked through.

>6 Drain well on kitchen paper. Transfer the pieces of fish to a plate and spear with wooden cocktail sticks.

Serve immediately with the sauce for dipping.

anchovies with chorizo & fennel

serves 8

ingredients

100 g/3½ oz chorizo
1 fennel bulb, trimmed and very thinly chopped
2 tsp fennel seeds
pinch of dried chilli flakes, or to taste
4 large tomatoes, peeled, deseeded and roughly chopped
Spanish olive oil, for brushing
8 fresh anchovies, heads removed and gutted
salt and pepper
lemon wedges, to serve

>1 Remove and discard the casing from the chorizo, then chop.

>2 Add the chorizo to a large, dry frying pan over a high heat and fry, stirring, for 3–5 minutes, until it gives off its fat.

>3 Add the fennel, reduce the heat to medium and fry, stirring, for 5–8 minutes, until soft.

>4 Add the fennel seeds and chilli flakes and stir for a further minute.

>5 Add the tomatoes and season to taste with salt and pepper.

>6 Simmer for 15–20 minutes, stirring occasionally, until the tomatoes break down and a sauce forms.

>7 Meanwhile, preheat the grill to high. Brush the grill pan with oil. Add the anchovies, sprinkle with salt and grill on each side for 2 minutes, or until cooked through and tender.

>8 Transfer the anchovies to a chopping board and cut each one into two fillets, removing the bones.

Divide the sauce between eight small bowls and arrange two anchovy fillets on top of each. Serve with lemon wedges for squeezing over.

calamares fritos

serves 6

ingredients
450 g/1 lb prepared squid
plain flour, for dusting
sunflower oil, for deep-frying
sea salt
lemon wedges and aïoli, to serve

>1 Slice the squid into 1-cm/½-inch rings and halve the tentacles if large.

>2 Dust the squid with flour so that it is lightly coated.

Sprinkle the fried squid with sea salt. Serve piping hot with lemon wedges for squeezing over and aïoli for dipping.

>3 Heat enough oil for deep-frying in a large saucepan or deep-fat fryer to 180–190°C/350–375°F, or until a cube of bread browns in 30 seconds. Carefully add the squid, in batches, and fry for 2–3 minutes, or until golden brown. Do not overcook.

>4 Using a slotted spoon, remove the fried squid from the oil and drain well on kitchen paper. Keep hot in a warm oven while you fry the remaining squid.

seafood croquettes

makes 24

ingredients

5 tbsp Spanish olive oil, plus extra for deep-frying
70 g/2½ oz plain flour
400 ml/14 fl oz milk
225 g/8 oz prepared cooked seafood, such as cod, hake, clams, prawns, salmon and salt cod, any skin and bones removed, very finely chopped
finely grated rind of 1 lemon
75 g/2¾ oz fine dry white breadcrumbs
1 large egg, beaten with 1 tbsp water
salt and pepper

>1 Heat the 5 tablespoons of oil in a saucepan over a medium heat. Gradually stir in the flour and continue stirring for 2 minutes.

>2 Remove from the heat and gradually stir in the milk, stirring constantly to prevent lumps from forming. Return the pan to the heat and bring to the boil, stirring until the sauce is smooth and thick.

>3 Stir in the seafood and lemon rind and season to taste with salt and pepper. Transfer to a bowl and leave to cool. Cover the surface with clingfilm and chill for at least 4 hours or overnight.

>4 Use wet hands to divide the seafood mixture into 24 balls. Wet your hands again, then roll the balls into 5 cm/2 inch long cork shapes.

>5 Put the breadcrumbs into a shallow bowl. One by one, dip the croquettes in the egg mixture and then roll in the breadcrumbs, turning until coated.

>6 Heat enough oil for deep-frying in a large saucepan or deep-fat fryer to 180–190°C/350–375°F, or until a cube of bread browns in 30 seconds.

>7 Add the croquettes to the pan, in batches, and fry for 2–2½ minutes, until golden brown.

>8 Transfer to a plate lined with kitchen paper and keep hot in a warm oven until all the croquettes are cooked.

Serve immediately while still warm.

sweet peppers stuffed with crab salad

makes 16

ingredients

1 red pepper
1 tsp Spanish olive oil
240 g/8½ oz canned crabmeat, drained and squeezed dry
1½ tbsp lemon juice, or to taste
200 g/7 oz cream cheese
16 pimientos del piquillo, drained
salt and pepper
chopped fresh parsley, to garnish

>1 Preheat the oven to 200°C/400°F/Gas Mark 6. Brush the red pepper with the oil and put in a roasting tin.

>2 Roast the red pepper in the preheated oven for 30 minutes, turn over and roast for a further 10 minutes, until the skin has blistered and blackened.

>3 Using a slotted spoon, transfer the roasted pepper to a polythene bag and leave for 15 minutes, or until cool enough to handle.

>4 Peel, core and deseed the pepper, then chop the flesh.

>5 Put half the crabmeat in a food processor with the red pepper, lemon juice, and salt and pepper to taste. Process until well blended, then transfer to a bowl.

Stir in the cream cheese and the remaining crabmeat. Taste and add extra lemon juice, if needed.

>7 Pat the pimientos with kitchen paper to dry and scoop out any seeds that remain in the tips.

Use a small spoon to divide the crab salad equally among the peppers, stuffing them generously.

Arrange on a large serving dish. Sprinkle with chopped parsley and serve.

scallop & serrano ham skewers

makes 4

ingredients
2 tbsp lemon juice
3 tbsp Spanish olive oil
2 garlic cloves, finely chopped
1 tbsp chopped fresh parsley
12 shelled scallops, with corals
8 wafer-thin slices Serrano ham
pepper

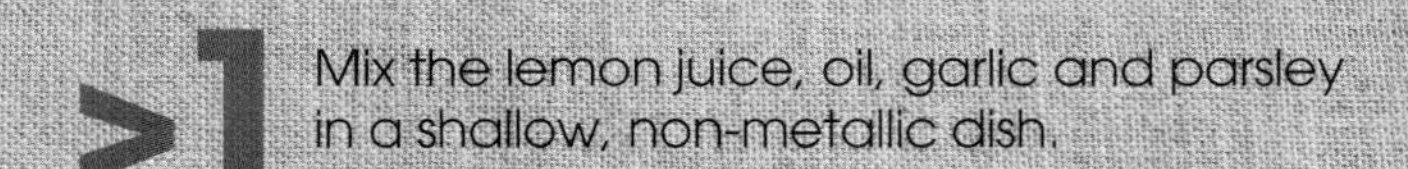

>1 Mix the lemon juice, oil, garlic and parsley in a shallow, non-metallic dish.

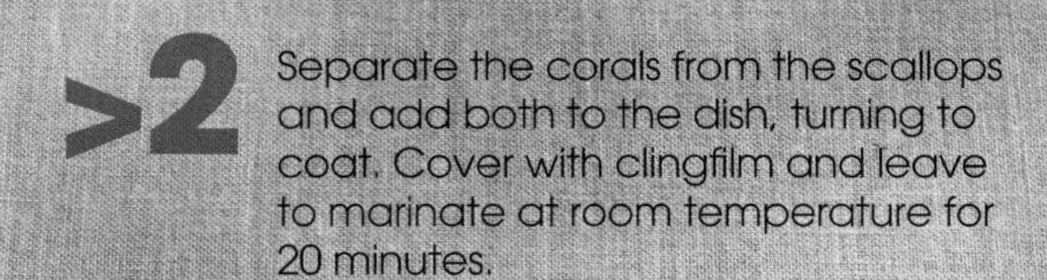

>2 Separate the corals from the scallops and add both to the dish, turning to coat. Cover with clingfilm and leave to marinate at room temperature for 20 minutes.

Transfer to warmed serving plates, sprinkle with pepper and serve immediately.

>3 Preheat the grill to medium. Drain the scallops. Thread a scallop and a coral onto a metal skewer. Scrunch up a slice of ham and thread it onto the skewer, followed by another scallop and a coral. Repeat to fill four skewers, each with three scallops and two slices of ham.

>4 Cook the skewers under the preheated grill, turning frequently, for 5 minutes, or until the scallops are tender and the ham is crisp.

tuna & red pepper empanada

serves 8

ingredients

2 tbsp Spanish olive oil
1 onion, chopped
4 large garlic cloves, finely chopped
400 g/14 oz canned chopped tomatoes
400 g/14 oz canned tuna, drained and flaked
2 large grilled red peppers in oil, drained and chopped
salt and pepper

pastry

450 g/1 lb strong white flour
1 sachet (7 g/¼ oz) easy-blend dried yeast
1 tsp salt
1 tsp sugar
125 ml/4 fl oz milk
40 g/1½ oz butter, plus extra for greasing
4 tbsp water
beaten egg, for glazing

>1 Preheat the oven to 190°C/375°F/ Gas Mark 5. Grease a baking sheet.

>2 To make the pastry, sift the flour, yeast, salt and sugar into a bowl. Make a well in the centre.

>3 Heat the milk, butter and water in a saucepan until the butter melts, stirring. Pour the liquid into the flour and mix to a soft, sticky dough.

>4 Turn out the dough onto a work surface and knead for 5–10 minutes, until smooth. Shape into a ball, cover and leave to rise until doubled in size.

>5 Heat the oil in a large frying pan, add the onion and fry for 3 minutes. Add the garlic and tomatoes, bring to the boil and boil for 5–8 minutes, mashing the tomatoes with a spoon, until reduced. Stir in the tuna and red peppers and season to taste with salt and pepper.

>6 Knock back the dough and divide in half. Roll one piece into a 30-cm/12-inch square and place on the prepared baking sheet. Spread the filling to within 1 cm/½ inch of the edge. Brush the edge with water.

>7 Roll out the remaining dough in the same way. Use to cover the filling, then seal the edges with a fork. Cut a small steam hole in the centre and bake in the preheated oven for 20 minutes.

>8 Remove from the oven and glaze with the beaten egg, then bake for a further 15 minutes, until golden.

Leave to stand for 10 minutes, then cut into bite-sized pieces. Serve warm or at room temperature.

salt cod fritters with spinach

serves 6

ingredients

250 g/9 oz dried salt cod in 1 piece
140 g/5 oz plain flour
1 tsp baking powder
¼ tsp salt
1 large egg, lightly beaten
100–150 ml/3½–5 fl oz milk
2 lemon slices
2 fresh parsley sprigs
1 bay leaf
½ tbsp garlic-flavoured olive oil
85 g/3 oz fresh baby spinach, rinsed
¼ tsp Spanish paprika
Spanish olive oil, for shallow-frying
sea salt, for sprinkling
aïoli (see page 64), to serve

>1 Put the salt cod into a large bowl, cover with cold water and leave to soak for 48 hours, changing the water at least three times a day.

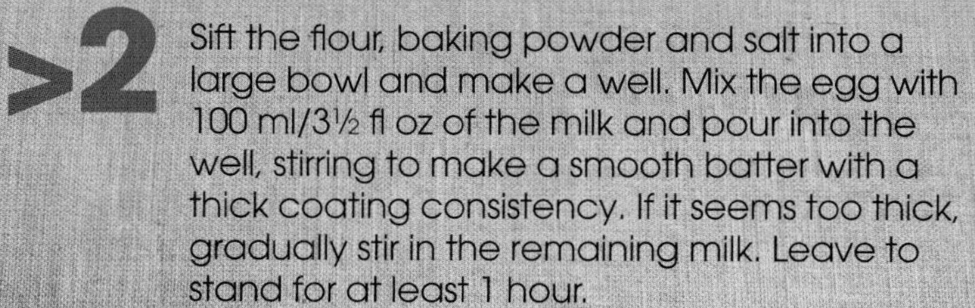

>2 Sift the flour, baking powder and salt into a large bowl and make a well. Mix the egg with 100 ml/3½ fl oz of the milk and pour into the well, stirring to make a smooth batter with a thick coating consistency. If it seems too thick, gradually stir in the remaining milk. Leave to stand for at least 1 hour.

>3 Drain the salt cod and transfer to a large frying pan. Add the lemon slices, parsley sprigs, bay leaf and enough water to cover and bring to the boil. Reduce the heat and simmer for 30–45 minutes, until the fish is tender and flakes easily.

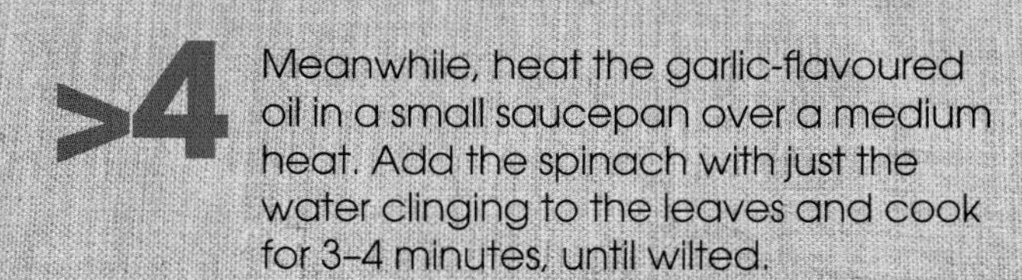

>4 Meanwhile, heat the garlic-flavoured oil in a small saucepan over a medium heat. Add the spinach with just the water clinging to the leaves and cook for 3–4 minutes, until wilted.

>5 Drain the spinach in a sieve, using the back of a spoon to press out any excess liquid. Finely chop the spinach, then stir it into the batter with the paprika.

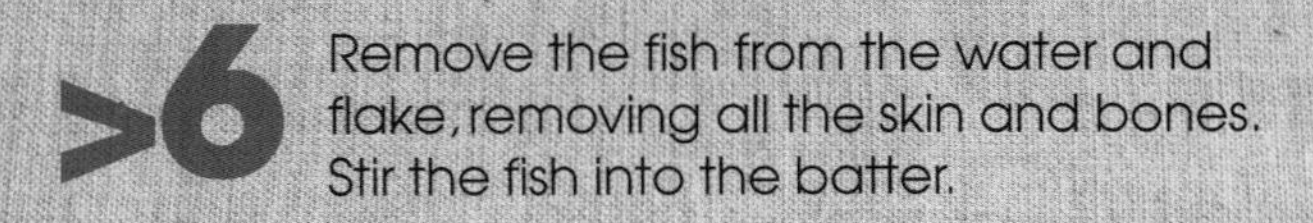

>6 Remove the fish from the water and flake, removing all the skin and bones. Stir the fish into the batter.

>7 Heat enough olive oil for shallow frying in a large frying pan. Use a greased tablespoon to drop spoonfuls of the batter into the oil and fry for 8–10 minutes, until golden brown. Work in batches to avoid overcrowding the pan.

>8 Use a slotted spoon to transfer the fritters to kitchen paper to drain.

Sprinkle with sea salt and serve hot or at room temperature with aïoli for dipping.

clams with saffron & lemon dressing

serves 8

ingredients

2 tbsp lemon juice
1 tsp honey
finely grated rind of 1 lemon
large pinch of saffron threads, soaked for 30 minutes in 2 tsp boiling water
4 tbsp Spanish extra virgin olive oil
1 kg/2 lb 4 oz live clams, rinsed
2 tbsp Spanish olive oil
1 onion, finely chopped
2 garlic cloves, finely chopped
125 ml/4 fl oz dry white wine
salt and pepper
slices of bread from a long, thin loaf, to serve

>1 Add the lemon juice, honey, lemon rind, and salt and pepper to taste to the infused saffron threads. Whisk in the extra virgin olive oil.

>2 Discard any clams with broken shells and any that refuse to close when tapped.

Transfer the clams to a serving dish and pour over the saffron and lemon dressing. Serve immediately with plenty of bread.

>3 Heat the olive oil in a large saucepan over a medium heat. Add the onion and garlic and fry for 3–5 minutes, until soft. Add the clams and wine, cover the pan and cook, shaking the pan, for 3–5 minutes, until the clams have opened. Discard any clams that remain closed. Strain the clams, reserving the cooking liquid.

>4 Return the cooking liquid to the pan and add the saffron mixture. Bring to the boil and boil until reduced by half.

fresh salmon with red pepper sauce

serves 6

ingredients

2 red peppers
700 g/1 lb 9 oz salmon fillet
4 tbsp Spanish olive oil, plus extra for brushing
1 onion, roughly chopped
1 garlic clove, finely chopped
6 tbsp dry white wine
100 ml/3½ fl oz double cream
salt and pepper

>1 Preheat the oven to 200°C/400°F/Gas Mark 6. Brush the red peppers with oil and put in a roasting tin.

>2 Roast the peppers in the preheated oven for 30 minutes, then turn over and roast for a further 10 minutes, until the skins have blistered and blackened.

>3 Using a slotted spoon, transfer the roasted peppers to a polythene bag and leave for 15 minutes, or until cool enough to handle.

Meanwhile, remove the skin from the salmon fillet and cut the flesh into 2.5-cm/1-inch cubes. Season to taste with pepper and set aside.

>5 Heat 2 tablespoons of the oil in a large frying pan, add the onion and cook, stirring occasionally, for 5 minutes, or until soft but not brown. Add the garlic and cook, stirring, for 30 seconds, until soft. Add the wine, bring to the boil and leave to bubble for 1 minute. Remove from the heat.

>6 Peel, core and deseed the peppers, then put the flesh into a food processor.

>7 Add the onion mixture and cream and process to a smooth purée. Season to taste with salt and pepper. Pour into a saucepan and gently heat.

>8 Heat the remaining oil in a frying pan. Add the salmon cubes and cook, turning occasionally, for 8–10 minutes, until cooked through and golden brown on all sides.

Transfer the salmon to a serving plate and serve with the sauce on the side.

monkfish escabeche

serves 8

ingredients

250 ml/9 fl oz Spanish extra virgin olive oil
1 large onion, thinly sliced
2 carrots, thinly sliced
4 large garlic cloves, thinly sliced
3 bay leaves
1–2 fresh green chillies, to taste, deseeded and thinly sliced
1 tbsp coriander seeds, crushed
250 ml/9 fl oz red wine vinegar or sherry vinegar
125 ml/4 fl oz dry white wine
750 g/1 lb 10 oz monkfish fillets
salt and pepper
chopped fresh coriander, to garnish

>1 Heat 125 ml/4 fl oz of the oil in saucepan over a medium heat. Add the onion and carrots and fry, stirring, for 8–10 minutes, until the vegetables are very tender but not brown.

>2 Add the garlic, bay leaves, chillies and coriander seeds and stir for 2 minutes. Season to taste with salt and pepper.

>3 Stir in the vinegar and wine and bring to the boil, then simmer for 10 minutes. Cover and keep warm.

>4 Meanwhile, using a small knife, remove the thin, grey membrane from the monkfish.

>5 Cut the monkfish into bite-sized pieces.

>6 Heat half the remaining oil in a large frying pan over a medium heat. Fry half the monkfish pieces, turning once, for 3–5 minutes, until just cooked through. Repeat until all the monkfish has been cooked.

>7 Drain well on kitchen paper and transfer to a non-metallic dish.

>8 Pour the warm vegetable mixture and the oil left in the pan over the fish. Leave to cool completely, then cover and chill for at least 36 hours and up to five days.

Sprinkle with chopped coriander and serve chilled or at room temperature.

mussels with paprika

serves 8

ingredients

1 kg/2 lb 4 oz live mussels, scrubbed and debearded
4 tbsp Spanish olive oil
1 large fennel bulb, trimmed and very finely chopped
4 large garlic cloves, finely chopped
1 tbsp tomato purée
2 tsp Spanish hot or sweet paprika, to taste
250 ml/9 fl oz dry white wine
salt and pepper
sliced country-style bread, to serve

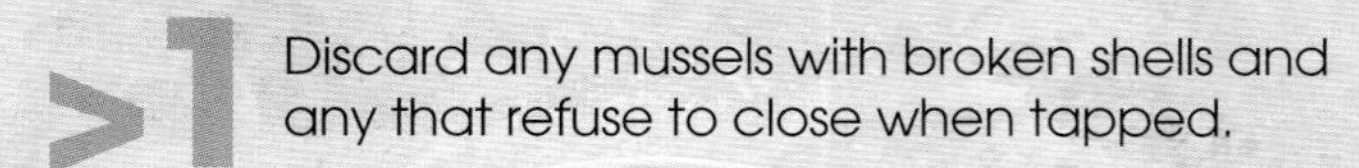

>1 Discard any mussels with broken shells and any that refuse to close when tapped.

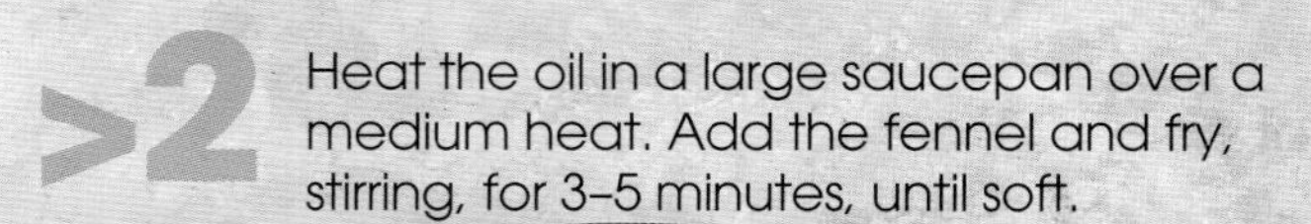

>2 Heat the oil in a large saucepan over a medium heat. Add the fennel and fry, stirring, for 3–5 minutes, until soft.

Remove the top shells, then transfer the mussels to a serving dish and pour over the cooking juices. Serve with plenty of bread.

>3 Stir in the garlic, tomato purée and paprika, reduce the heat and stir for a further minute. Pour in the wine and bring to the boil, stirring, until the liquid is reduced by half.

>4 Reduce the heat, then add the mussels, cover the pan and steam for 3–5 minutes, until they open. Discard any mussels that remain closed. Season to taste with salt and pepper.

meat & poultry

chorizo in red wine

serves 6

ingredients

200 g/7 oz chorizo
200 ml/7 fl oz Spanish red wine
2 tbsp brandy
fresh flat-leaf parsley sprigs, to garnish
crusty bread, to serve

>1 Use a fork to prick the chorizo a few times. Place the chorizo and wine in a large saucepan. Bring the wine to the boil, then reduce the heat, cover and simmer gently for 15–20 minutes.

>2 Transfer the chorizo and wine to a bowl, cover and leave to marinate for 8 hours or overnight.

>3 Drain the chorizo, reserving the wine. Remove the outer casing from the chorizo and cut the sausage into 5-mm/¼-inch slices. Place the chorizo slices in a large, heavy-based frying pan.

>4 Pour the brandy into a small saucepan and heat gently.

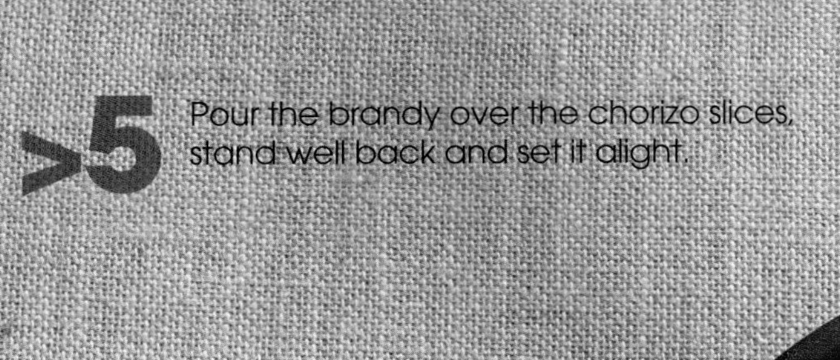

>5 Pour the brandy over the chorizo slices, stand well back and set it alight.

>6 When the flames have died down, gently shake the pan, add the reserved wine and cook over a high heat until almost all of the wine has evaporated.

Serve piping hot, garnished with parsley sprigs and accompanied by bread.

tiny meatballs in almond sauce

serves 6

ingredients

55 g/2 oz white or brown bread, crusts removed
3 tbsp water
450 g/1 lb fresh lean pork mince
1 large onion, finely chopped
1 garlic clove, chopped
2 tbsp chopped fresh flat-leaf parsley, plus extra to garnish
1 egg, beaten
freshly grated nutmeg
plain flour, for coating
2 tbsp Spanish olive oil
lemon juice, to taste
salt and pepper

almond sauce
2 tbsp Spanish olive oil
25 g/1 oz white or brown bread, broken into pieces
115 g/4 oz blanched almonds
2 garlic cloves, finely chopped
150 ml/5 fl oz dry white wine
425 ml/15 fl oz vegetable stock
salt and pepper

>1 Put the bread into a bowl, add the water and leave to soak for 5 minutes. Using your hands, squeeze out the water and transfer the bread to a dry bowl.

>2 Add the pork, onion, chopped garlic, parsley and egg, then season to taste with nutmeg and salt and pepper. Knead well to form a smooth mixture.

>3 Spread some flour on a plate. Using floured hands, shape the meat mixture into about 30 equal-sized balls, then roll each meatball in flour until coated.

>4 Heat the oil in a large, heavy-based frying pan. Add the meatballs, in batches if necessary, and fry for 4–5 minutes, or until brown on all sides. Using a slotted spoon, remove the meatballs from the frying pan and set aside.

>5 To make the sauce, heat the oil in the same pan. Add the bread and almonds and gently fry, stirring frequently, until golden brown.

>6 Add the finely chopped garlic and fry for a further 30 seconds, then pour in the wine and boil for 1–2 minutes. Season to taste with salt and pepper and leave to cool slightly.

>7 Transfer the bread and almond mixture to a food processor. Add the stock and process until smooth. Return to the pan.

>8 Carefully add the meatballs to the sauce and simmer for 25 minutes, or until tender. Taste the sauce and season with salt and pepper if needed.

Transfer to a warmed serving dish, add a squeeze of lemon juice to taste and garnish with chopped parsley. Serve immediately.

asparagus wrapped in ham

makes 16

ingredients

16 asparagus spears
8 thin slices Serrano ham, cut in half lengthways
Spanish olive oil, for brushing
salt
aïoli (see page 64), to serve

>1 Hold each asparagus spear at each end and bend until the woody stalk snaps. Discard the broken ends.

>2 Bring a frying pan of lightly salted water to the boil. Lay as many asparagus spears in the pan as will fit in a single layer. Bring back to the boil, then turn off the heat, cover and leave to steam for 3–5 minutes, until just tender.

Transfer to a serving platter. Serve warm or at room temperature with aïoli for dipping.

>3 Use tongs to transfer the asparagus to a bowl of iced water. Repeat with any remaining spears. Pat the asparagus dry and wrap a piece of ham around each spear.

>4 Heat a ridged griddle pan over a high heat. Lightly brush with oil. Add as many asparagus spears as will fit in a single layer and fry, turning occasionally, for 3–5 minutes, until the ham is crisp. Repeat until all the spears have been cooked.

crispy chicken & ham croquettes

makes 8

ingredients

4 tbsp Spanish olive oil
4 tbsp plain flour
200 ml/7 fl oz milk
115 g/4 oz cooked chicken, minced
55 g/2 oz Serrano ham, very finely chopped
1 tbsp chopped fresh flat-leaf parsley
small pinch of freshly grated nutmeg
1 egg, beaten
55 g/2 oz day-old white breadcrumbs
sunflower oil, for deep-frying
salt and pepper
aïoli (see page 64), to serve

>1 Heat the olive oil in a saucepan over a medium heat. Stir in the flour to form a paste and cook gently for 1 minute, stirring constantly.

>2 Remove the pan from the heat and gradually stir in the milk until smooth. Return to the heat and slowly bring to the boil, stirring constantly, until the mixture boils and begins to thicken.

>3 Remove the pan from the heat, add the chicken and beat until the mixture is smooth. Add the ham, parsley and nutmeg and mix well. Season to taste with salt and pepper.

>4 Spread the chicken mixture in a dish and leave for 30 minutes until cool, then cover and chill for 2–3 hours or overnight.

>5 Divide the chicken mixture into eight portions. Use wet hands to form each portion into a cylindrical shape.

>6 Pour the beaten egg onto a plate and put the breadcrumbs on a separate plate. Dip the croquettes, one at a time, in the beaten egg, then roll in the breadcrumbs to coat. Chill for at least 1 hour.

>7 Heat enough sunflower oil for deep-frying in a large saucepan or deep-fat fryer to 180–190°C/350–375°F, or until a cube of bread browns in 30 seconds. Add the croquettes, and deep-fry for 5–10 minutes, or until golden brown and crisp.

>8 Remove the croquettes with a slotted spoon and drain well on kitchen paper.

Serve the croquettes piping hot, accompanied by aïoli for dipping.

andalusian pork skewers

makes 16

ingredients

900 g/2 lb boneless lean pork loin chops, about 1 cm/½ inch thick
2 large garlic cloves, finely chopped
2 tsp Spanish sweet paprika
2 tsp ground cumin
¼ tsp ground cinnamon
pinch of cayenne pepper, or to taste
4 tbsp Spanish olive oil, plus extra for brushing
2 tsp tomato purée
1 green pepper, deseeded and cut into 16 squares
salt and pepper
lemon wedges, to serve

>1 Cut the pork into 32 bite-sized pieces.

>2 Combine the garlic, paprika, cumin, cinnamon, cayenne pepper, and salt and pepper to taste in a large bowl. Stir in the oil and tomato purée.

>3 Add the pork and rub the marinade into the meat. Cover and chill for at least 8 hours or overnight.

>4 About 30 minutes before cooking, soak 16 wooden short skewers in cold water. Preheat the grill to high and brush the grill pan with oil.

>5 Bring a saucepan of water to the boil. Add the green pepper pieces and blanch for 1 minute. Drain and rinse under cold running water. Pat dry and set aside.

Thread a piece of pork onto a cocktail stick, then add a piece of green pepper and another piece of pork. Repeat to make 16 skewers.

>7 Arrange the skewers on the prepared grill pan and brush with any remaining marinade.

Grill for 12–15 minutes, turning frequently, until the pork is cooked through and lightly charred.

Serve immediately with lemon wedges for squeezing over.

chorizo & broad beans

serves 8

ingredients

1 kg/2 lb 4 oz fresh broad beans, shelled, or 350 g/12 oz frozen broad beans
250 g/9 oz chorizo
2 tbsp finely chopped fresh parsley
salt and pepper
Spanish extra virgin olive oil and sliced crusty bread, to serve

>1 Bring a saucepan of lightly salted water to the boil over a high heat. Add the broad beans, bring back to the boil and cook for 5–8 minutes for fresh beans, or for 4–5 minutes for frozen beans, until tender.

>2 Meanwhile, cut the chorizo in half lengthways. Remove and discard the casing, then thinly slice.

Transfer to a serving bowl and drizzle with extra virgin olive oil. Serve hot or at room temperature with plenty of bread.

>3 Drain the beans and immediately transfer them to a bowl of iced water. Use your fingers to pop the beans out of their skins, then pat dry and set aside.

>4 Put the chorizo into a dry frying pan over a medium–high heat and cook, stirring, for 3–5 minutes, until it gives off its fat. Add the beans and stir until heated through. Stir in the parsley and season to taste with salt and pepper.

beef skewers with orange & garlic

makes 8

ingredients

3 tbsp white wine
2 tbsp Spanish olive oil
3 garlic cloves, finely chopped
juice of 1 orange
450 g/1 lb rump steak, cubed
450 g/1 lb baby onions, halved
2 orange peppers, deseeded and cut into squares
225 g/8 oz cherry tomatoes, halved
salt and pepper

>1 Mix together the wine, oil, garlic and orange juice in a shallow, non-metallic dish.

>2 Add the beef, season to taste with salt and pepper and toss to coat.

>3 Cover with clingfilm and leave to marinate in the refrigerator for 2–8 hours.

>4 Preheat the grill to high. Drain the beef.

>5 Thread the beef, onions, orange peppers and tomatoes alternately onto eight metal skewers.

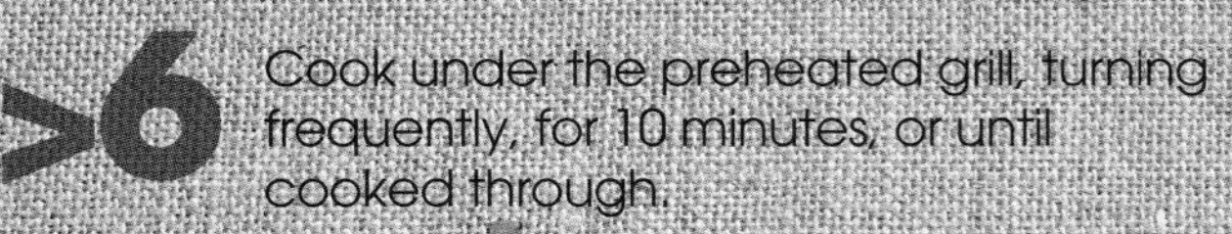

>6 Cook under the preheated grill, turning frequently, for 10 minutes, or until cooked through.

Transfer to warmed serving plates and serve immediately.

paella-stuffed tomatoes

makes 16

ingredients

large pinch of saffron threads
500 ml/18 fl oz chicken stock
100 g/3½ oz chorizo
1 onion, finely chopped
4 large garlic cloves, finely chopped
250 g/9 oz skinless, boneless chicken thighs, finely diced
125 g/4½ oz fine French beans, trimmed and finely chopped
1 yellow pepper, deseeded and finely chopped
2 tsp Spanish hot paprika
250 g/9 oz Spanish paella rice
16 tomatoes
salt and pepper

>1 Put the saffron in a dry frying pan and toast over a high heat, stirring, for 30 seconds–1 minute, until it is giving off its aroma. Immediately tip it into a saucepan, add the stock and bring to the boil. Remove from the heat, cover and set aside.

>2 Remove and discard the casing from the chorizo and finely dice.

>3 Add the chorizo to a large dry frying pan over a high heat and fry, stirring, for 3–5 minutes, until it gives off its fat.

>4 Add the onion and garlic to the pan. Reduce the heat and fry, stirring occasionally, for 5–8 minutes, until soft. Add the chicken, French beans, yellow pepper and paprika and stir for a further 2 minutes.

>5 Add the rice and gently stir until it is coated with the oil. Pour in the stock and saffron mixture, season to taste with salt and pepper and bring to the boil without stirring.

>6 Reduce the heat to very low and simmer for 20–25 minutes, uncovered, until the rice is tender and all the liquid has been absorbed. Shake the pan occasionally but do not stir.

>7 Meanwhile, cut a very thin sliver off the bottom of each tomato, so it can stand upright. Cut off the tops and use a small spoon to scoop out and discard the seeds. Sprinkle with salt and leave to drain upside down.

>8 Leave the paella to stand for 5 minutes, then spoon it into the tomato shells.

Arrange the tomatoes upright on a serving dish and serve hot or at room temperature.

chicken wings chilindron

makes 16

ingredients
16 chicken wings, wing tips cut off
4 tbsp Spanish olive oil
1 large onion, finely chopped
1 large green and 1 large red pepper, deseeded and chopped
100 g/3½ oz Serrano ham diced
4 large garlic cloves, finely chopped
800 g/1 lb 12 oz canned chopped tomatoes
2 bay leaves
1 tbsp dried thyme
125 ml/4 fl oz water
1 tsp Spanish hot paprika
salt and pepper

>1 Season the chicken wings with salt and pepper. Heat the oil in a large, heavy-based frying pan over a medium heat, then add the chicken wings, in batches, and fry on both sides until golden brown. Remove from the pan and set aside.

>2 Add the onion, peppers, ham and garlic to the pan and cook for 5–8 minutes, until the onion is soft.

Transfer to a large serving platter and serve immediately.

>3 Stir in the tomatoes, bay leaves, thyme and water and season with salt and pepper. Bring to the boil, then reduce the heat, cover and simmer for 15 minutes, stirring occasionally.

>4 Stir in the paprika and chicken wings, making sure they are covered with the sauce. Cover and simmer for 15–20 minutes, until the chicken wings are tender and the juices run clear when a skewer is inserted into the thickest part of the meat.

pork belly bites

serves 8

ingredients

- 900 g/2 lb boneless pork belly, skin scored
- 2 fennel bulbs, trimmed and halved
- 8 black peppercorns, crushed
- 4 garlic cloves, sliced
- 125 ml/4 fl oz dry white wine
- salt
- romesco sauce (see page 60), to serve

>1 Preheat the oven to 150°C/300°F/Gas Mark 2. Put the pork, skin-side up, into a large flameproof casserole. Add the fennel, peppercorns, garlic and wine, and season to taste with salt.

>2 Pour over enough water to cover the pork. Bring to the boil, then cover and transfer to the preheated oven. Cook for 5½ hours, until the pork is tender.

>3 Remove from the oven, take off the lid and leave the pork to cool in the cooking liquid for 30 minutes.

>4 Carefully transfer the pork to a chopping board that will fit in the refrigerator. Discard the cooking liquid.

>5 Cover the pork with a baking sheet and put several food cans on top. Leave the pork to cool completely. Transfer to the refrigerator and leave overnight.

>6 Preheat the oven to 180°C/350°F/ Gas Mark 4. Line a baking sheet with baking paper. Very carefully trim the pork and cut into bite-sized pieces.

>7 Put as many pork pieces as will fit, skin-side down, into a non-stick frying pan and fry for 6–8 minutes, until the fat runs. Increase the heat to medium–high and fry for a further 5 minutes, until the skin is crisp and brown. Repeat with any remaining pieces.

>8 Transfer the pork to the prepared baking sheet, skin-side up. Roast in the preheated oven for 20 minutes, until hot.

Transfer the pork to a serving plate and spear with wooden cocktail sticks. Serve hot with romesco sauce for dipping.

pork empanadas

makes 16

ingredients

4 tbsp Spanish olive oil, plus extra for greasing
1 red onion, finely chopped
115 g/4 oz chorizo, casing removed, finely chopped
250 g/9 oz fresh pork mince
4 large garlic cloves, finely chopped
1 tbsp dried thyme
400 g/14 oz canned chopped tomatoes
flour, for dusting
1 quantity empanada pastry (see page 150), rolled out to a thickness of 3 mm/⅛ inch on a floured board
egg yolk, for glazing
salt and pepper

>1 Heat the oil in a large frying pan over a medium heat. Add the onion and fry until soft. Add the chorizo, pork, garlic and thyme and season to taste with salt and pepper. Fry, breaking up the meat with a wooden spoon, until brown.

>2 Add the tomatoes to the pan, stir and simmer until reduced.

>3 Preheat the oven to 190°C/375°F/Gas Mark 5. Lightly grease a baking sheet.

>4 Dip an 11-cm/4½-inch cutter in the flour and use to cut out 16 rounds from the dough, re-rolling as necessary.

>5 Hold each dough round in your hand and add 2 teaspoons of the filling. Wet the edge, then fold into a half-moon shape and press to seal. Press the tines of a fork all around the edge.

>6 Transfer the empanadas to the prepared baking sheet. Beat the egg yolk and use to brush the tops of the empanadas, then make a small steam hole in each. Bake in the preheated oven for 15–20 minutes, until golden brown and puffed.

Leave to cool on the baking sheet for at least 5 minutes, then serve warm or at room temperature.

sirloin steak with garlic & sherry

serves 6–8

ingredients

4 sirloin steaks, about 175–225 g/6–8 oz each and 2.5 cm/1 inch thick
5 garlic cloves
3 tbsp Spanish olive oil
125 ml/4 fl oz dry Spanish sherry
salt and pepper
chopped fresh flat-leaf parsley, to garnish
crusty bread, to serve

>1 Trim the fat from the steaks. Cut the steaks into 2.5-cm/1-inch cubes and place in a large, shallow dish.

>2 Slice three of the garlic cloves and set aside. Finely chop the remaining garlic cloves and sprinkle over the steak. Season generously with pepper and mix well. Cover and chill for 1–2 hours.

Garnish with chopped parsley and serve hot with bread to mop up the juices.

>3 Heat the oil in a large frying pan, add the garlic slices and cook over a low heat, stirring, for 1 minute, or until golden brown. Increase the heat, add the steak and cook, stirring constantly, for 2–3 minutes, until browned.

>4 Add the sherry and cook until reduced Season to taste with salt and transfer to a warmed serving dish.

chicken livers in sherry sauce

serves 6

ingredients

450 g/1 lb chicken livers, trimmed
2 tbsp Spanish olive oil
1 small onion, finely chopped
2 garlic cloves, finely chopped
100 ml/3½ fl oz dry Spanish sherry
2 tbsp chopped fresh flat-leaf parsley, plus extra sprigs to garnish
salt and pepper
country-style bread or toast, to serve

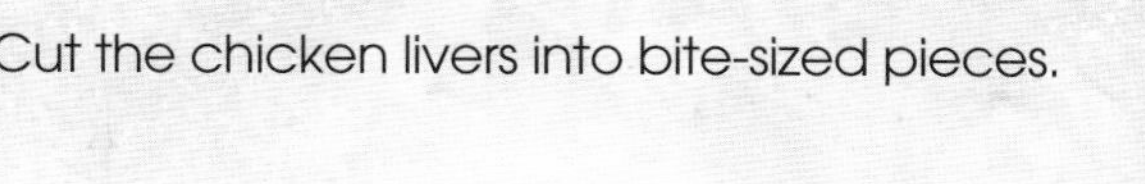

>1 Cut the chicken livers into bite-sized pieces.

>2 Heat the oil in a large, heavy-based frying pan. Add the onion and fry for 5 minutes, or until soft but not brown. Add the garlic and fry for a further 30 seconds.

>3 Add the chicken livers to the pan and fry for 2–3 minutes, stirring constantly, until they are firm and have changed colour on the outside but are still pink the centre.

>4 Using a slotted spoon, lift the chicken livers from the pan and transfer to a warmed serving dish.

>5 Add the sherry to the pan, increase the heat and leave it to bubble for 3–4 minutes to reduce slightly. Deglaze the pan by scraping up all the bits on the base of the pan into the sauce with a wooden spoon. Season to taste with salt and pepper.

Pour the sauce over the chicken livers and sprinkle over the chopped parsley.

Garnish with parsley sprigs and serve piping hot with bread.

chicken rolls with olives

serves 6–8

ingredients

115 g/4 oz black Spanish olives in oil, drained and 2 tbsp oil reserved

140 g/5 oz butter, softened

4 tbsp chopped fresh parsley

4 skinless, boneless chicken breasts

>1 Preheat the oven to 200°C/400°F/Gas Mark 6. Stone and finely chop the olives. Mix together the olives, butter and parsley in a bowl.

>2 Place the chicken breasts between two sheets of clingfilm and gently beat with a meat mallet or the side of a rolling pin.

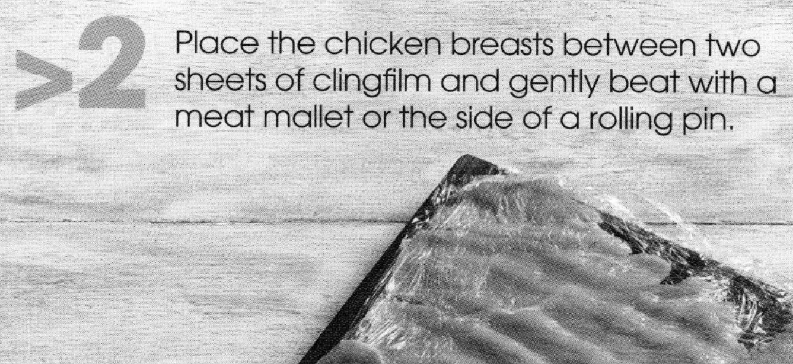

>3 Spread the olive and parsley butter over one side of each flattened chicken breast and roll up.

>4 Secure with wooden cocktail sticks or tie with kitchen string.

>5 Place the chicken rolls in an ovenproof dish. Drizzle over the reserved oil from the olives and bake in the preheated oven for 25–30 minutes, or until tender and the juices run clear when a skewer is inserted into the thickest part of the meat.

>6 Transfer the chicken rolls to a chopping board, discard the cocktail sticks or string and slice with a sharp knife.

Transfer to a warmed serving plate and serve immediately.

chargrilled lamb chops & peppers

serves 8

ingredients
4 tbsp Spanish olive oil, plus extra for brushing
2 tbsp red wine vinegar or sherry vinegar
2 large garlic cloves, finely chopped
1 tbsp sugar
1 tbsp chopped fresh thyme leaves
2 tsp chopped fresh oregano leaves
16 baby lamb chops, ribs well trimmed
4 red peppers, deseeded and quartered
salt and pepper

>1 Combine the oil, vinegar, garlic, sugar, thyme and oregano in a large, non-metallic bowl. Add the lamb chops and rub with the mixture. Cover and leave to marinate at room temperature for up to 2 hours.

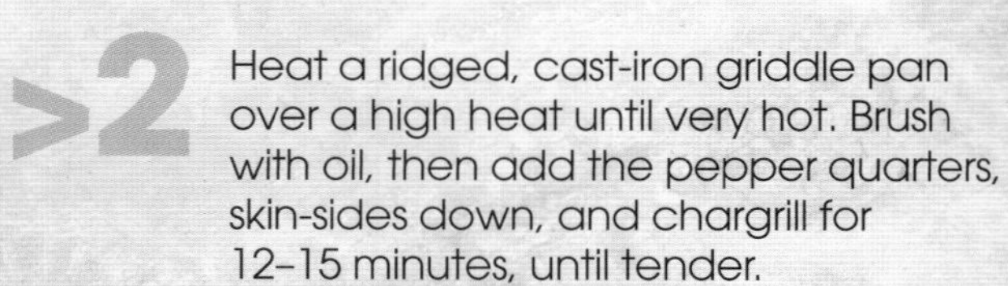

>2 Heat a ridged, cast-iron griddle pan over a high heat until very hot. Brush with oil, then add the pepper quarters, skin-sides down, and chargrill for 12–15 minutes, until tender.

Arrange the red pepper strips on a serving platter and top with the lamb chops. Serve hot, warm or at room temperature.

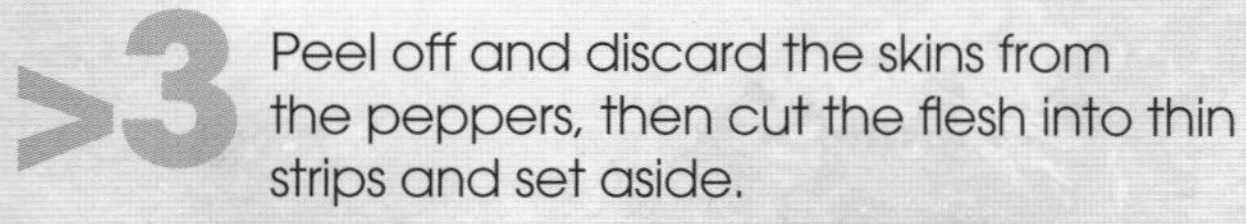

>3 Peel off and discard the skins from the peppers, then cut the flesh into thin strips and set aside.

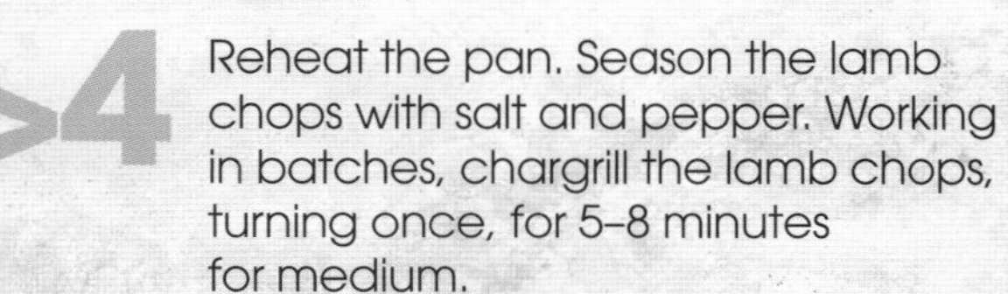

>4 Reheat the pan. Season the lamb chops with salt and pepper. Working in batches, chargrill the lamb chops, turning once, for 5–8 minutes for medium.

Index